Five Critical
Leadership Practices

What are the critical practices of leaders in high-performing schools? Based on extensive observations, interviews, and in-depth case studies of principals and superintendents who significantly increase student learning and achievement, this exciting new book provides novice and veteran school leaders with the five critical steps for effective school leadership:

1. Focus on Direction
2. Build a Powerful Organization
3. Ensure Student-Focused Vision and Action
4. Give Life to Data
5. Lead Learning

Rich with voices from highly effective leaders, this book provides an accessible, research-based framework for school improvement that is correlated with the field's standards. The engaging case studies in this vital resource show the power of these five key critical practices to make a difference in the lives of students and transform schools to support learning for all.

Ruth C. Ash is a long-time educator, a nationally known consultant in the areas of education, leadership, and organizational effectiveness, and a Founding Partner of Education Solutions.

Pat H. Hodge is a lifelong educator, working with administrators and teachers in developing student-focused instructional practices and cultures, and a Founding Partner of Education Solutions.

Other Eye On Education Books Available from Routledge
(www.routledge.com/eyeoneducation)

What Connected Educators Do Differently
Todd Whitaker, Jeffrey Zoul, and Jimmy Casas

BRAVO Principal! Building Relationships with Actions that Value Others, 2nd Edition
Sandra Harris

Get Organized! Time Management for School Leaders, 2nd Edition
Frank Buck

The Educator's Guide to Writing a Book: Practical Advice for Teachers and Leaders
Cathie E. West

Data, Data Everywhere: Bringing All the Data Together for Continuous School Improvement, 2nd Edition
Victoria Bernhardt

Leading Learning for Digital Natives: Combining Data and Technology in the Classroom
Rebecca J. Blink

The Trust Factor: Strategies for School Leaders
Julie Peterson Combs, Stacey Edmonson, and Sandra Harris

The Assistant Principal's Guide: New Strategies for New Responsibilities
M. Scott Norton

The Principal as Human Resources Leader: A Guide to Exemplary Practices for Personnel Administration
M. Scott Norton

Formative Assessment Leadership: Identify, Plan, Apply, Assess, Refine
Karen L. Sanzo, Steve Myran, and John Caggiano

Easy and Effective Professional Development: The Power of Peer Observation to Improve Teaching
Catherine Beck, Paul D'Elia, and Michael W. Lamond

Job-Embedded Professional Development: Support, Collaboration, and Learning in Schools
Sally J. Zepeda

Leading Schools in an Era of Declining Resources
J. Howard Johnston and Ronald Williamson

Creating Safe Schools: A Guide for School Leaders, Teachers, and Parents
Franklin P. Schargel

Data Analysis for Continuous School Improvement, 3rd Edition
Victoria Bernhardt

What Great Principals Do Differently: 18 Things That Matter Most, 2nd Edition
Todd Whitaker

Five Critical Leadership Practices

The Secret to High-Performing Schools

Ruth C. Ash and Pat H. Hodge

Routledge
Taylor & Francis Group

NEW YORK AND LONDON

First published 2016
by Routledge
711 Third Avenue, New York, NY 10017

and by Routledge
2 Park Square, Milton Park, Abingdon, Oxon, OX14 4RN

Routledge is an imprint of the Taylor & Francis Group, an informa business

© 2016 Taylor & Francis

Library of Congress Cataloging in Publication Data
Names: Ash, Ruth C., author. | Hodge, Pat H., author.
Title: Five critical leadership practices : the secret to high-performing schools / Ruth C. Ash, Pat H. Hodge.
Description: New York, NY : Routledge, 2016. | Includes bibliographical references.
Identifiers: LCCN 2015027141| ISBN 9781138889248 (hardback) | ISBN 9781138889255 (pbk.) | ISBN 9781315713021 (ebook)
Subjects: LCSH: Educational leadership—United States. | School management and organization—United States. | School improvement programs—United States. | Academic achievement—United States.
Classification: LCC LB2805. A68 2016 | DDC 371.2—dc23LC record available at http://lccn.loc.gov/2015027141

ISBN: 978-1-138-88924-8 (hbk)
ISBN: 978-1-138-88925-5 (pbk)
ISBN: 978-1-315-71302-1 (ebk)

Typeset in Optima
by Keystroke, Station Road, Codsall, Wolverhampton

Contents

Preface

Why Do We Care about This Topic?

Effective leadership does not occur by happenstance. Successful leadership is seldom easy. Truly effective school and district leaders demonstrate practices that transform schools into true learning environments for everyone. Since all leaders benefit from learning successful strategies from their peers, why not share their secrets? As leaders guide faculty in developing their practice, school cultures change, and students learn at ever deeper levels. No longer does surface learning substitute for meaningful learning of substantive content. Through an examination of current leadership research, coupled with extensive observations and interviews with leaders whose schools and districts demonstrated substantial improvement in student learning, the following five leadership practices emerged as critical:

1. Focus on Direction
2. Build a Powerful Organization
3. Ensure Student-Focused Vision and Action
4. Give Life to Data
5. Lead Learning

For Whom Did We Write This Book?

We wrote it for you. We examined several formats for communicating our message to an audience including school leaders, district leaders and policy makers, higher education leadership professors, and other groups working to make a difference in learning for all—students and faculty. Creating a student-focused learning environment requires leaders to develop an understanding of key practices critical to successful collaborative learning communities as well as those crucial to transforming the entire organization. Within this book is a guide for leaders who strive to change or deepen a culture of student-focused learning that, ultimately, requires changes in practices for all stakeholders, especially faculty and staff. As leaders implement the Five Critical Practices, student learning increases.

What Is Our Goal for Writing This Book?

We live in a time where super heroes are ever present in the metroplex and where we seemingly look to our leaders—both political and some-times spiritual—to be almost superhuman, and yet wait for the latest tabloid exposé to prove that they are not. This book tells stories of extraordinary leaders who with exceptional support accomplish amazing results. They are stories of successful collaborations that begin with strong relationships. Simply putting staff together in a room does not create trust or develop relationships. Developing trust among peers is primary to productive relationships and successful collaboration. In this book, we highlight needed structures and parameters for the creation of risk-free environments that support collaboration among colleagues. The book stresses five essential practices for creating and sustaining a culture that values looking at old problems in new ways, thinking outside of the building—not just out of the box—and setting aside or giving up former routines that interfere with a culture of collaboration. The goal for this book is to support leaders when faced with challenges that interfere with student learning.

What Is the Organization of This Book?

We organized the book into five sections that describe each of the Five Critical Practices of effective leaders who increase student learning. Each practice includes standards and indicators that expand the understanding of the practices.

Focus on Direction

Effective principals and superintendents focus on the identified direction of the organization and maintain clear expectations for collegial collaboration to improve student learning. An effective leader facilitates the identification of core beliefs about teaching and learning and commits to making decisions through the filter of those beliefs. The mission, vision, and beliefs guide all decisions and actions within the organization.

Build a Powerful Organization

Effective leaders pose the question: what is best for students? As stakeholders respond to the question, their answers help frame new organizational processes for decision-making. They create environments that encourage high levels of learning and support faculty and staff in risking new practices, often stepping considerably out of their comfort zones. Effective leaders constantly nurture leadership abilities in others. The organization and leadership create an environment of shared responsibility, which leads to the common goal of improvement in all areas.

Ensure Student-Focused Vision and Action

Effective leaders of high-performing schools and districts guide stakeholders in basing their actions on student-focused visions for the school. Effective principals and superintendents model student-focused procedures that concentrate on the advancement of student learning rather than on adult preferences. A driving emphasis on students and their learning maintains the focus on direction, involves everyone, and supersedes all other initiatives.

Give Life to Data

Effective leaders base decisions on data that focus on results. They lead faculty and staff in decision-making processes driven by data. These processes include careful selection of appropriate data for analysis, gathering the data, disaggregating and analyzing the data, and managing the use of the data. The use of data as a decision-making tool identifies the strengths and weaknesses of students and the organization as a whole.

Lead Learning

As the world continuously changes and evolves, the educational environment changes to meet exploding expectations. These changes provide no easy answers and require that educational leaders, faculty, and the greater educational community expand their abilities and knowledge of students and learning. Effective leaders in high-performing organizations understand the need for reflection to remain diligent in their leadership roles as they support an environment that fosters collaboration and daily learning for all. A crucial role of effective leaders is to guide schools and districts through positive and productive change. These leaders grasp the unqualified importance of helping others appreciate the ongoing need for flexibility and change.

In Summary . . .

This work is the culmination of decades spent teaching, researching, studying, facilitating, observing, and leading the pursuit of practices that result in increased learning for all. Thorough and current research from the field formed the premise for the foundation and assumptions of the book. To communicate its message effectively, we provide authentic examples to expand the commentary. Additionally, *Tips for Leaders* accompany each section with concrete practices to support the work. Our format for communicating these practices is through case studies. Numerous principals and superintendents are "change agents" within their communities, and we appreciate the willingness of a few who shared their stories of creating high-performing schools and districts.

Acknowledgments

We thank our husbands, Chuck and Will, for their support and understanding of all the times we were not available over the last several years. As our biggest cheerleaders and first outside readers of this book, we are grateful.

A special thanks to Monica Solomon for her valuable comments as an outside reader and encouragement as a colleague. Monica personifies a culture of sharing. Many thanks also to Peggy Connell for her support throughout the process.

We owe a huge debt of gratitude to Routledge/Taylor & Francis Publishers, especially Heather Jarrow, for encouraging us to write this book. Your support, guidance, feedback, and patience throughout the process made a daunting task less intimidating. The experience pushed us to fine-tune our thoughts, beliefs, and commitments about the critical nature of leadership in any organization, but particularly in education. Thank you.

To each of the leaders in the case study schools and districts, your generosity in sharing your time, practices, journeys, and data reflects the true collaborative spirit so necessary for real growth and change to occur in education. Collectively, principals, faculty, superintendents, and other supporters of learning have the knowledge to transform our schools. The power is in the sharing! We celebrate your many successes, and applaud your willingness to share your disappointments so that all may learn. As we share our knowledge, we collaborate as colleagues in the task of changing our schools from places of teaching to places of learning.

Introduction

Effective leaders demonstrate practices that transform schools and districts into institutions of learning and improve student performance while maintaining an eye on past experiences, present circumstances, and future opportunities (Kearney et al., 2013). Through extensive observations, surveys, interviews, site visits, and personal communications, authors Ash and Hodge identified school and district leaders with the shared belief that their role was to help people think differently about student learning. The direct quotations from leaders are taken from the personal communications, which are listed at the end of the References.

These leaders lived the belief that schools can make a difference in the lives of students and in the life of communities.

The Five Critical Practices

This book shares the case studies of leaders who significantly increased student learning and an analysis of research regarding leader effectiveness. The common findings among these leaders confirm the following Five Critical Practices and skills of effective leadership to improve student learning:

Critical Practice 1: Focus on Direction
Critical Practice 2: Build a Powerful Organization
Critical Practice 3: Ensure Student-Focused Vision and Action

Critical Practice 4: Give Life to Data
Critical Practice 5: Lead Learning

The Five Critical Practices consistently surfaced in case studies of the leadership practices of highly effective leaders.

Creating Transformation through the Critical Practices

Over the last four decades, educators experienced seemingly endless negative comments about ill-equipped teachers and the dire state of education in the United States. The media often provided opportunities for individuals to expound on the decline of education and the need for a solution. However, this book is the story of what happens in schools when effective, forward-thinking leaders collaborate with their staffs in the difficult task of creating change-adaptive learning environments with a *focus on learning* rather than a *focus on teaching*.

George Hall Elementary School

When *Terri Tomlinson* became principal of George Hall Elementary School in Mobile, Alabama, it was among the worst performing schools in Alabama, with fewer than 50% of the fourth-graders performing at grade level in reading or mathematics. The demographics of the school painted an all too familiar picture of students caught in a never-ending cycle of poverty leading nowhere.

Mrs. Tomlinson transferred voluntarily from the principalship in a high-performing elementary school to George Hall. The school's low academic levels over a period of years prompted the district to remove the entire faculty and charge Mrs. Tomlinson with hiring all new faculty. With the exception of three teachers, Mrs. Tomlinson recruited a whole new team. The transformation and investment in the school's success involved everyone—faculty, aides, custodians, and cafeteria workers. All participated in planning, decision-making, and training, and all knew the daily math and reading themes and questioned students in the cafeteria and halls about math and reading. Faculty and staff in every area had high expectations for students, each other, and themselves.

Going door-to-door to visit parents, Mrs. Tomlinson and her assistant principal built a new level of trust within the community. Their efforts resulted in a new commitment to the school and a renewed belief in the education potential of George Hall.

Fast-forward six years to find a considerable increase in student achievement. After the implementation of many instructional and organizational changes by Mrs. Tomlinson and her staff, George Hall received numerous national awards and recognition for high student performance and innovative teaching.

Alice Ott Middle School

When *James Johnston* first came to Alice Ott Middle School as principal, student expectations and achievement were low. There were significant achievement gaps among special education, English-language, economically disadvantaged, and White students. He said, "There was no shared mission, no clear picture of what quality literacy instruction meant; no strategic plan to help struggling readers; and worst of all, no understanding of who was struggling."

Johnston's first step was to get faculty input about what needed to occur. First, they spent some time talking about other organizations' visions and missions. For example, they studied Nike's mission, which is "To bring inspiration and innovation to every athlete in the world," and how Nike has used it to create success. They also discussed how the private sector uses branding to make improvements. Then, different groups wrote down their ideas, people voted on the ideas, and they developed Alice Ott's mission "To provide a safe, challenging, and supportive environment where students are prepared with the fundamentals for success in high school and beyond, developing them into responsible citizens and critical thinkers" and the school motto: "Champions find a way!"

After identifying the mission of the school, Principal Johnston led the staff in determining steps to achieve the mission.

"Our school is different now," Johnston said. "People believe— students, teachers, parents have confidence. Now we believe that we will make it." And they are making it. Alice Ott was in the top 10%

of the schools in the state, an achievement that won them the designation as an Oregon Model School for three years in a row. Alice Ott was named a 2014 MetLife–NASSP Breakthrough School for its academic success and a 2015 Title I Distinguished School for helping low-income students succeed and closing achievement gaps. Principal Johnston received the 2013 Oregon Middle School Principal of the Year award, and Vice Principal Duane Larson is Oregon's 2015 Vice Principal of the year.

Maplewood Richmond Heights High School

Kevin Grawer, principal of Maplewood Richmond Heights High School in St. Louis, Missouri, believed that *when students felt cared for, their learning increased significantly*. "It is our job," he said, "to see that they do." He told the students, faculty, and staff every day that he loved them and told the students that he would not let them fail. He and his faculty visited every home and "got to know the students and their families as individuals." Mr. Grawer led the entire Maplewood faculty in participating in risk-free working teams. Some of the teams were an intervention team, a literacy team, a professional development team, a building advisory team, a teaching and learning committee that also included parents, and an honors committee. The teams met regularly and often to examine solutions to problems and perform the organizational work of the school. They also served as successful models of collaboration for students. Kevin Grawer received recognition as a Walsworth Consummate Professional in 2012. Student achievement and ACT averages showed significant increases, and Maplewood Richmond Heights High School was named a 2013 MetLife–NASSP Breakthrough School for its academic success.

Within the Five Critical Practices, Tomlinson, Johnston, and Grawer used a variety of methods to make the extensive and significant changes that transformed their schools. Their methods are described in later chapters in the book, along with many other case studies of schools and school districts struggling with the same issues. Each school or district demonstrated significant gains in student achievement over time. The case studies provide a view in greater depth of the practices of these leaders and their staffs and describe how they intuitively or deliberately modeled the Five

Critical Practices of effective leaders, which resulted in success for the students and schools.

The Need for Change: Addressing the Global Educational Gap

The transformations of George Hall, Alice Ott, Maplewood Richmond Heights, and the others in this book stand as examples of what education in America needs to accomplish without delay. According to U.S. Secretary of Education Arne Duncan (2010), "The hard truth is that other high-performing nations have passed us by during the last two decades . . . The gap between top-performing countries and the U.S. is meaningful—and large" (para. 17).

It is a disturbing reality that many students in America fail to perform at their highest academic levels. For example, even though over one million low-income elementary-school students rank in the top quartile on nationally normed standardized tests, significantly fewer maintain their high-achieving status throughout their school years than do higher income students (Wyner et al., 2007). In addition, America's top students do not compare well to those from many other countries. In mathematics, for example, "only 2% of students in the United States reach the highest level (Level 6) of performance in mathematics, compared with an Organization for Economic Co-Operation and Development average of 3% and 31% of students in Shanghai-China" (Organization for Economic Co-operation and Development, 2012).

Good news abounds, however! Considerable current research and best practices demonstrate that leaders make a substantial difference in student achievement (Leithwood et al., 2004; Waters et al., 2003). The Mid-Continent Research for Education and Learning's meta-analysis identified 21 leadership responsibilities that correlate significantly with higher student achievement (Waters et al., 2003). The Wallace Foundation's work in the area of school leadership included a six-year study that identified how successful educational leadership improves student learning and recognized five practices that define successful leadership (Wallace Foundation, 2012). Several national organizations also identified standards that defined the traits that characterized effective principals, or their actions, or their knowledge and understanding. The Interstate School

Leaders Licensure Consortium (ISLLC) formulated six standards, with each standard undergirded by explanatory subsets in the categories of Knowledge, Dispositions, and Performances (ISLLC, 2012). The National Association of Elementary School Principals (2008) organized six standards around leading learning communities. The National Association of Secondary School Principals (2010) identified "10 skills for successful school leaders." The Southern Regional Education Board (2010) organized 13 critical success factors into three key competencies.

The Five Critical Practices outlined in this book correlate with the major standards and practices identified by these organizations and synthesize the findings.

Which changes in actions and practices will increase student learning? How will the educational community improve instructional practices so that the whole of student learning is greater than the sum of the parts? Current research indicates that the talents and competences of the organizational leader powerfully influence the transformation and outcome of the organization (Leithwood et al., 2004; Waters et al., 2003).

> In essence, the principal is probably the most essential element in a highly successful school. The principal is necessary to set change into motion, to establish the culture of change and a learning organization, and provide the support and energy to maintain the change over time until it becomes a way of life in the school . . . Without high-quality leadership, high-quality schools cannot exist.
>
> (Valentine et al., 2004, p. 112)

Waters and Marzano (2007) found that district leadership is related to student achievement. Effective superintendents collaborate to set firm goals, monitor goals for teaching and learning, and make sure resources are available for achieving the district's goals.

Five Critical Leadership Practices is a book written for a critical time when many American students have fallen woefully behind their global peers in performance and when bad news of every kind seems to be everywhere. But this is a *good news book* that tells many exceptional stories of *extraordinary leaders who make the critical difference in the lives of students and frequently in the life of their communities*. These effective educators shared their *secrets to high-performing schools and school districts* as models that can be adapted by other educational leaders engaged in *learning for all*.

Critical Practice 1

Focus on Direction

To paraphrase from a conversation between Alice and the Cheshire Cat in Lewis Carroll's *Alice in Wonderland*, "If you don't know where you are going, any road will take you there" (Carroll, 2004).

High-performing schools and school districts are crystal clear about what they do, why they do it, and what results they want to achieve. Everyone—students, faculty, staff, and parents—can describe what the organization is about and where it needs to grow. There is a vibrant focus on direction at every level and in every area. Leaders in schools and school districts with a strong focus on direction intentionally create an organizational culture that is supportive of all learners, work with everyone to ensure high-quality performance, and use the vision, mission, and strategic plan to make decisions.

2 | Creating an Organizational Culture

Every school and district has a culture. At issue is whether the culture, unintended, has developed over time into a fragmented and misaligned environment or whether leaders shape the culture to support communication, collaboration, improvement, trust, and learning. Leaders of high-performing schools and districts make a deliberate decision to create the kind of culture that enables all the areas necessary for staff and student engagement and success. They create a culture of caring, communication, and collaboration that has positive stakeholder relationships and that builds trust and supports diversity.

Creating an organizational culture is difficult. It involves bringing together diverse people with different ideas and beliefs and their own comfortable ways of doing things. It is not something a leader can accomplish overnight, but requires time and patience and, at the same time, a willingness to push people beyond their own comfort levels.

Deal and Peterson (1999, p. 1) state: "The culture of an enterprise plays the dominant role in exemplary performance." Intentionally establishing an organizational culture that includes facilitating conversations among stakeholders may be one of a leader's most critical responsibilities in ensuring success.

Creating a Shared Culture of Caring, Communication, and Collaboration

Leaders of high-performing organizations create a culture of three Cs— caring, communication, and collaboration. Superintendents and principals who establish this kind of positive culture provide an environment that enables success for everyone. Relationships with caring teachers have a significant effect on student achievement (Montalvo et al., 2007). Open communication and collaboration among faculty provide "opportunities for adults across a school system to learn and think together about how to improve their practice in ways that lead to improved student achievement" (Annenberg Institute for School Reform, 2004, p. 2).

Tips for Leaders

- Develop family-like relationships among faculty, staff, students, and stakeholders. Create opportunities for sharing personal stories. Socialize after work or set up a way for others to socialize at lunch.

- Let everyone know they are valued for their unique contributions. Provide recognition and rewards for different kinds of contributions.

- Create opportunities for faculty to learn together about how to improve their practice through options such as common planning times, retreats, lesson studies, and critical friends groups. Ensure that there is enough time for collaboration.

- Everyone requires warmth and connection with others. Students need it. Teachers need it. When hiring faculty and staff, look for people who can create a caring and warm environment.

Principal Tomlinson and George Hall's faculty and staff achieved a stunning increase in student learning. She continually reflected a culture and climate of caring through her conversations and her actions. She communicated the value of creating a caring school community by comparing faculty, staff, and students to family members who take care of one another. Through relationships with her faculty, staff, students, and parents, she modeled and encouraged a culture of caring that extended beyond the school. Students have responded to this caring. According to a fourth-grade teacher,

> I knew my students would come with baggage. I didn't realize it would be every single child. My first year here (the second in the transformation), many of my students were overage, sometimes significantly. That is no longer the case. I used to have boys shove papers from their desk, cry openly, and throw major temper tantrums.

That doesn't happen anymore at all. Students used to walk with their heads down and suck their thumbs, even those as old as 10 and 11 years. I don't see that behavior at all anymore. Students are proud of themselves. They work hard and have tools to overcome obstacles. It isn't that students are perfect, or we as teachers are, but they understand and respect our common goal and know we are there for them.

George Hall's national recognition for its high student performance and innovative teaching remains a hallmark of its work. The school received several prestigious awards and recognitions for its high academic performance, including the National Renaissance Learning Lighthouse School of Excellence and recognition as one of three elementary schools in the nation to hold the title of 2012 Intel School of Distinction in mathematics. After the significant changes in George Hall's programs and processes, over 95% of the students met or exceeded grade-level standards in reading.

Effective change leaders "reframe change from an overwhelming and pervasive threat, to a modification of practice within the broader picture of affirming every colleague as a worthwhile professional and person" (Reeves, 2009, p. 7).

Kevin Grawer, principal of Maplewood Richmond Heights High School in St. Louis, Missouri, believed it was the leaders' responsibility to make sure that students knew their teachers and administrators cared about them. He continuously told the students, faculty, and staff that he loved them. Maplewood leaders and faculty demonstrated caring by visiting the home of every student. In Tomlinson's and Grawer's schools, the culture of caring, communication, and collaboration ensured high levels of student learning.

Developing Positive and Productive Relationships with Stakeholders

According to Henderson and Mapp (2002), a number of studies demonstrate the relationship between family involvement and increased student achievement. In addition, schools studied by Dorfman and Fisher (2002) exhibit higher levels of success when the curriculum promotes connections among communities, families, and students.

Alaska's Chugach School District (CSD) includes 22,000 square miles in communities around Prince William Sound and the mountains and islands near Anchorage. In addition to its schools, CSD includes a statewide homeschool program (FOCUS Homeschool) and a statewide variable-term residential school. In the early 1990s, CSD was in crisis; 90% of the students read below grade level and a significant percentage were not successful after high school. School staff and community members did not always trust each other. They clearly needed an out-of-the-box solution.

To identify and begin to address their many problems, CSD held regularly scheduled school meetings, town meetings, and business partner meetings to gather ideas about common beliefs and goals. CSD developed a community input process where faculty, administrators, community members, and students were trained to facilitate community meetings. The monthly meetings were co-facilitated by community members, students, and faculty for 2½ years in multiple communities. They used straightforward activities, such as asking community participants to think of someone successful and identify the characteristics of that successful person. Then they asked participants to determine which of those characteristics graduates needed to know and be able to do. They developed their shared vision and the first local performance standards from that community input. All stakeholders gave input into the strategic planning process.

At first, there was little engagement and not much trust. Superintendent *Bob Crumley* said:

> Many community members did not believe we would listen. We did listen, however, and we honored and used their input—and we publicly announced how their input had impacted the system. For example, community elders said we have an Alaskan native culture that has been ignored. We added cultural standards that are included in the curriculum for all students. Trust began to grow when community members saw the system was being developed based on their honest input.

The results of CSD's changes were extraordinary. In addition to significant achievement increases, the dropout rate decreased by almost half, and more than two-thirds of CSD's graduates entered college. Chugach High School received the national New American High School Award. CSD was selected as a recipient of Alaska's APEX Excellence Award, the highest state level of recognition for performance excellence, and was the first educational organization to win the Baldrige National Quality Award.

Tips for Leaders

- Develop a community input process, and make sure that every communication has a response from the school or district within a specific and *short* wait time. Use relevant community suggestions and make sure to publicize their use.
- Involve stakeholders in developing policies and procedures, and ensure transparency of the policies and procedures.
- Hold student-led parent and community meetings.
- Invite stakeholders to volunteer in the school, and engage them in discussions during the day.

Suzanne Freeman also understood the power of relationships. As the new superintendent for Pike Road Schools, a recently formed public school district in Pike Road, Alabama, Dr. Freeman realized the necessity of building a community of supporters for the fledging district. She devoted a year prior to opening the new school district to capturing the community's vision for their new schools. Freeman did not wait for stakeholders to come to her. She met them where they lived, worked, worshipped, played, or studied. The community focus meetings allowed Freeman to share her vision and beliefs about teaching and learning and gather valuable feedback from the community about their vision for their children.

Educators agree that positive and productive relationships with stakeholders are beneficial. These kinds of stakeholder relationships, however, take time to develop and maintain and create the most value when developed intentionally. This requires planning, trust, and open communication. Superintendents and principals cannot build constructive stakeholder relationships alone. The deepest and most productive stakeholder relationships require the commitment and communication of faculty and staff as well.

Facilitating Conversations among Stakeholders

Fostering community and parent support about the direction of the school or district and the renewed emphasis on student learning requires constant communication and collaboration with stakeholders. As educators, we have mastered the art of one-way communication, but to garner stakeholder support the communication must be reciprocal. Clearly, stakeholders talk with each other on a regular basis. However, it is in the interest of the school or district for educators to be a participant in those conversations and to facilitate further formal and informal discussions.

Tips for Leaders

- Communicate regularly through e-mail, newsletters, and websites, *incorporating a consistently reviewed and publicly shared method for stakeholder response.*
- Use social media to connect with stakeholders. Ask for stakeholder input concerning the effectiveness of the social media communication.
- Invite stakeholders to volunteer and engage them in discussions during the day.
- Provide training for stakeholders that they perceive as helpful, and involve them in assessing the training.
- Provide information on policies and procedures, and request feedback from stakeholders. Involve stakeholders in developing policies and procedures.
- Invite prospective stakeholders to school and district events.
- Institute regular community meetings.

Designing engaging conversations among varied groups of stakeholders can be challenging, but the rewards are many, including enhanced understanding among groups, improved relationships, positive participation in problem resolution, and increased future support for new initiatives.

Social media is indispensable now in business communication, and wise leaders take note of these methods of communication to facilitate conversations among stakeholders. At George Hall Elementary School, interested stakeholders can follow teachers' and leaders' tweets and send tweets in response. One parent's Twitter story demonstrated the benefits of technology. His son's teacher tweeted regularly about classroom happenings. One day she tweeted that they were studying turtles in science. The parents and child then had a rich and informed discussion at dinner about what he learned in class that day. Another tweet directed tweeters to an online site to watch George Hall's History of African American Music performed by the students.

Several leaders in these case study schools facilitated stakeholder conversations through student-led parent meetings that highlighted students' work. Generally, parents divided into rotating groups, and each group viewed a different type of student work. For example, one group might view a student-created website and post to a student-created blog. Other groups might participate in student-led discussions or student demonstrations of lessons. These conversations helped parents develop a greater understanding of the work of the students and the focus for the direction of the school in preparation for the 21st century workforce.

Encouraging and Modeling Conversations and Actions that Build Trust and Support Diversity

Trust is the basis for working together to achieve the mission and goals of any organization.

Just as the conversations and actions in CSD fostered trust and supported the community's diverse populations, leaders in high-performing schools and districts model and encourage this way of working. We recognize trust when we see it. Faculty, staff, and students say what is on their minds and feel free to take risks, even if efforts do not always succeed. People talk openly about what is and is not working and make collective decisions to change things that need to improve. People ask questions, even if they think the answers may not be what they want to hear. Faculty watch each other teach and ask for suggestions from their colleagues. We see trust in action in myriad ways in high-performing schools and districts.

Tips for Leaders

- Build trust through communicating openly, doing what you say you will do, trying to do the right thing, and getting to know staff personally.
- Sometimes simply asking stakeholders for input and taking their advice builds trust.

Bryk and Schneider (2002) found that trust was critical for increased student learning. High trust levels among teachers, between teachers and the principal, and between educators and parents, were correlated with reading and mathematics improvement. In fact, schools with these high levels of trust were three times more likely to show student-learning increases than those with low trust levels.

As America moves toward an ever more culturally diverse society, students need to learn how to interact regularly in positive, productive, and trusting ways with others who are different. Modeling the support of diversity is the *morally and ethically right thing to do*. It also creates practical benefits for students. Students who attend diverse schools exhibit deeper and richer levels of dialogue, less prejudice, and higher levels of critical thinking and problem solving. In fact, in problem solving activities, diverse student groups performed at a higher level than experts in a particular profession (Page, 2008). Attendance at diverse schools helps students understand the perspectives of others from different backgrounds, a skill needed for the collaborative work today's employers require.

Terri Tomlinson's co-workers may have questioned her decision to transfer from a high-achieving school to the high-poverty, low-performing George Hall Elementary School. Mrs. Tomlinson's conviction to provide high-level learning experiences for all students propelled her to accept the challenge. The freedom to recruit her own staff and develop a new school culture based on trust enabled her to create the caring, collaborative school climate necessary to implement significant and systemic change. The interviewing and hiring processes presented a platform for Mrs. Tomlinson to share her vision and high-performance expectations for students, faculty, and staff. She invited a diverse group of those individuals with similar philosophies and beliefs to join her as she transformed George Hall Elementary School.

As the first summer progressed, the team coalesced and determined their personal and collective beliefs and vision about teaching, learning, and equity for all students. Conversations were held within the community and provided opportunities for faculty and staff to understand the fears and frustrations of community members for their individual children and the school as a whole. These meetings also allowed the surrounding neighborhood to hear and learn the new goals and direction for the school and built trust between educators and community members.

Working with Others to Support, Encourage, or Require High Performance

Becoming a high-performing organization requires hard work, time, and people working together. Creating a high-performing organization will not occur in isolation, and the superintendent or principal working alone cannot do it. The best thinking of everyone involved or interested in the school or district—faculty and staff, students, parents, community members, and business partners—is a necessity.

In a high-performing organization, leaders work with others to set expectations; develop goals; create processes to monitor implementation; and provide feedback, direction, and support.

Setting Expectations that Promote High Levels of Performance in Every Area

> In a democracy, all citizens must develop a taste for excellence so that the judgments they make will lead to excellence rather than mediocrity.
>
> (Schlechty, 2009, p. 15)

Setting high expectations promotes high levels of performance. This is true of faculty, staff, and students in every area of a school or district—the classroom, the cafeteria, the office, and the team meeting room. Educators frequently think only of students or faculty when they discuss high expectations. These conversations often omit other staff members, such as custodians and bus drivers. High expectations can create a transformation in belief and behavior in every area, not only in the classroom.

Expectations for high performance require buy-in from everyone for successful implementation. Consequently, the establishment of expectations is a collaborative effort with faculty, staff, and other stakeholders, rather than the responsibility of the superintendent or principal alone.

Tips for Leaders

- Develop expectations for high performance collaboratively with staff and other stakeholders. Make sure that expectations cover every area—student work, teacher practice, administrator leadership, custodial work, cafeteria functions, etc.—and that everyone knows what the expectations are. Review and revise expectations as needed.
- Consider instituting home visits by administrators and staff to involve parents in student expectations.

Kipp Shine Prep in Houston, Texas, was an open-enrollment, public, college-preparatory school, which enrolled high-poverty students. At Kipp Shine Prep, high expectations were clear, with students attending school for 9 hours 45 minutes—from 7:25 am until 5:00 pm.

Before the school year started, faculty visited the home of every incoming student, and everyone—students, parents, and faculty—signed a "Commitment to Excellence" that listed the responsibilities of each person to help the student reach the goals. Incoming students also attended a weeklong summer session that outlined school expectations. Student expectations were displayed throughout the school and included "climb the mountain to college" and "work hard" and "be nice." Obtaining a college degree was an expectation for all students. At the end of each week, the school celebrated student learning and recognized student achievement.

The high expectations resulted in high student achievement. Kipp Shine Prep earned the highest Distinction Rating possible from the Texas Education Agency, five stars. The school earned distinction in several areas—Reading/ELA, Mathematics, Student Progress, Closing Performance Gaps, and

Postsecondary Readiness (Harvard Family Research Project, 2010; Kaplan and Chan, 2011).

High expectations at George Hall Elementary School involved everyone—administrators, faculty, and staff. They all participated in planning, decision-making, and all had high expectations for students, each other, and themselves. A fourth-grade teacher said:

> What I like about Hall is that there are no excuses. One teacher described it as meeting the students where they are, strapping a big belt around them all, and saying, "Here we go," until we are all across the finish line. I like that kind of determination about what is best for the students.

Ensuring that Everyone Has Actionable Improvement Goals

> Only leadership can motivate the actions needed to alter behavior in any significant way. Only leadership can get change to stick by anchoring it in the very culture.
>
> (Kotter, 1996, p. 30)

Strategic goals provide focus on what is important and necessary and support the effective and efficient use of time and resources. Without strategic goals, it is easy to concentrate on which objective or action is merely next in line, which is more interesting, or which is temptingly easiest. When goals are clear and actionable, everyone knows the priorities and expected actions. Effective leaders develop organizational goals collaboratively and ensure that all individuals in the school or district have their own goals.

Chugach School District (CSD) included everyone in the development of the district's organizational performance goals, five-year timeline, and one-year targets. The goals encompassed student learning, character development, student needs, transition skills, and technology. Every CSD student had individual learning plan goals and had a hand in developing them.

Tips for Leaders

Many organizations develop strategic goals classified as SMART goals. SMART can stand for several different goal descriptors, but usually represents:

- **S**—Specific
- **M**—Measurable
- **A**—Achievable
- **R**—Relevant
- **T**—Time-bound

When *Drew Cook* became principal of Garner Magnet High School in Garner, North Carolina, there were significant gaps between White, Black, and Hispanic students. The number of suspensions was high, and the percentage of students graduating was low.

Mr. Cook and faculty decided Garner Magnet could become a great school. They formed teams, including a leadership team, a school improvement team (SIT), an instructional support team (IST), and professional learning teams (PLTs), and focused on clear, actionable goals. Administrators and department chairs established the leadership team in order to review issues that affected the entire school and share their considerations with the faculty and staff. Faculty began working in PLTs that met weekly by content area to plan and implement improved curriculum and instruction. The SIT identified a task force for each of the school's goals and charged project managers with monitoring action steps and reporting the results.

After these and many other changes, in addition to student achievement increases, the four-year graduation rate increased considerably. Garner Magnet was named a US News and World Report Bronze Medal Winner in 2012, 2013, and 2014 and named a 2014 MetLife–NASSP Breakthrough School for its academic success (NASSP, 2013). Drew Cook is now Senior Director of High School Programs for the Wake County School District.

Establishing Processes to Monitor Implementation of Expectations and Goals

Tips for Leaders

- Collaboratively develop processes to ensure implementation of goals and expectations. For example, teams could meet several times throughout the year and talk about what worked and what did not work. A regular faculty meeting could be dedicated to goal review.

- Conduct after-action reviews. The after-action review (AAR) captures lessons learned from successes and failures to apply to future actions. An AAR can be frequent, brief, informal process checks or more formal in-depth assessments. There are several critical steps in conducting an AAR:
  - Hold the AAR immediately after the activity.
  - Identify a facilitator.
  - Create an open, inviting climate where people feel free to discuss their ideas.
  - Identify the gap between the anticipated outcome and the actual outcome. Discuss what needs to be changed, and develop an action plan.

Processes ensure regular and ongoing monitoring. Without established processes, monitoring is often sporadic and ineffective. Administrators, faculty, and staff should collaboratively design the processes that monitor the implementation of expectations and goals. Possible processes might include an individual's review of their own goal completion, student and parent feedback, or a team's assessment of its results.

Processes that monitor the effectiveness of expectations and goals reveal the level of success in meeting the goals and expectations. Schools and districts deepen their effectiveness as they implement processes regularly, share them widely, and ensure understanding by all.

Several school and district leaders convened their leadership teams shortly after the last day of school to reflect upon the year and monitor the achievement of expectations and goals. They discussed such questions as: *What went well? What could we do to improve? Is there anything we should stop doing or start doing?* They identified strategies and areas for growth at that time, and began again the process for continuous improvement.

At Alice Ott Middle School in Portland, Oregon, students spoke 32 different languages. As a result, the principal, James Johnston, and faculty developed a school-wide focus on literacy development across content areas. Their goal was for all students to be on or above grade level by the end of eighth grade. Literacy team members led two meetings per year for follow-up on the school-wide literacy development goal. After faculty used specific literacy best practices, they shared the results in the meetings, discussed what worked and what did not work, and identified needed changes. "I don't think you can leave anything to chance," Johnston said.

Providing Feedback, Direction, and Support to Strengthen Performance and Mentor Emerging Leaders

Tips for Leaders

- Mentor new leaders. Offer opportunities for leadership, but include guidance. Set goals and try new activities. (Be sure to discuss failures as learning experiences.)
- Use resource groups such as mentoring circles, so new leaders can learn from each other and form a network.
- Identify ways to free time for teacher-leaders to observe teacher-leaders in other schools.

Leaders of high-performing schools and districts build on and develop the leadership capacity of all individuals involved in improving teaching and learning. They work consistently to create a partnership of shared responsibility for a common goal. According to Timothy Waters and the coauthors of *Balanced leadership* (2009, p. 8), "The future demands on the school principal are massive. In order to meet the needs of all stakeholders, the principal needs to learn to share leadership responsibilities while understanding the implications of introducing change."

Effective leaders create an environment that supports teachers as leaders and allows administrators to be facilitators of teacher-leaders' performance and growth. An important and vital point to remember is that shared leadership and mentoring emerging leaders is not delegation. Delegation is simply giving an assignment to someone else to accomplish. Mentoring others toward a path of leadership and sharing leadership involves coaching, encouraging, giving direction, providing support, offering feedback, and sharing wisdom.

At Maplewood Richmond Heights High School, everyone took responsibility for student learning. Faculty leadership roles included rewriting the curriculum, designing and leading professional development, and helping hire new faculty. A faculty team built capacity by creating protocols, identifying effective practices, and giving feedback to colleagues.

Phyllis Faust, principal of Hewitt-Trussville Middle School in Trussville, Alabama, inducted new faculty members into the leadership culture deliberately. Each group member joined a cohort, and the most recently hired cohort met monthly with Dr. Faust. Assistant principals and individual faculty members led each of the two previous years' cohorts. All cohorts participated in book studies, with members facilitating discussions. The three-year experience of each cohort allowed participants the time and protected environment to develop and demonstrate their leadership skills in a safe and secure setting. According to Dr. Faust, developing the leadership capacity of all individuals is "all about the relationships."

Using a Vision, Mission, and Strategic Plan to Make Decisions and Inform Actions

At its most basic, strategic planning generally includes identification of beliefs, mission, and vision of the organization; a review of the current and past strengths and weaknesses; organized goal setting; and action planning for the future. The problem with many strategic plans is that they often collect dust on whatever shelf they inhabit, and, even if reviewed regularly, they fail to transform strategy into action. To overcome this, the most effective plans focus on a collaboratively developed vision and mission; include practices, possibly outside the norm, that are consistent with the vision and mission; and support the direction of the organization.

Strategic plans provide a clear direction for everyone to work toward student success. With a strategic plan, everyone is thinking about the same goals. With the right kind of strategic plan, a school or district is able to better meet the challenges of the rapidly changing educational environment.

Collaborating with Others to Develop a Mission, Vision, and Strategic Plan That Reflect the Beliefs, Ethics, and Focus of the Organization

A mission, vision, and strategic plan that add value to the organization require collaborative development. Collaborative development ensures alignment of the vision, mission, and strategic plan to beliefs and ethics and to the focus of the organization. This alignment is critical to the success of plans, processes, actions, and results. In general, *more alignment translates into a higher level of success.*

Tips for Leaders

- To develop a vision, use the *People* magazine activity. Tell the group: It is now the year 2030, and your school or school district has accomplished everything you most wanted. You have become so successful that *People* magazine featured you as its cover story in this week's issue. Describe what this cover story says. Some suggestions for your description:
  - What picture is on the cover?
  - What are the headlines?
  - What are the human interest stories and quotes?
- Use an affinity diagram (see Appendix A) to develop the mission statement.

An organization's vision is a shared image, not of the current reality but of the hopes of those involved (Kotter, 1996). The vision is the best future imagined for all students. A vision statement explains, for the future, where the organization is going and the expectations for its purpose. A mission statement is a proclamation of the core purpose or overall function of the organization. For schools or districts, it answers three questions:

- What are we trying to accomplish?
- What services do we provide?
- What is important to us?

A compelling vision and a clear, meaningful mission inspire support and loyalty for the school or district. These vision and mission statements are encouraging, moving, and motivating when developed collaboratively and shared with everyone.

Craig Bates is the former principal of Winterboro High School in Talladega County, Alabama. He is currently the coordinator of instructional technology for the entire district. When Mr. Bates became principal of Winterboro, the school had lost focus and no longer met the academic standards that were a hallmark of its history. He began a powerful collaboration to develop a vision and mission. He used this effort to challenge the status quo and lead everyone in changing the environment of the school from one of *doing what we've always done* to one of building on the interests and strengths of every student and providing alternate avenues for learning and success through project-based learning. Student performance increased significantly. Discipline referrals, out-of-school suspensions, and alternative school referrals decreased, and the graduation rate increased. Mr. Bates described the changes as an evolutionary process in culture, climate, and commitment resulting in Winterboro High School receiving the prestigious National School Change Award, one of only six schools in the country to win this award in 2012.

Mr. Bates shared his sense of urgency about the students with faculty, staff, students, parents, and others. He further made the commitment to support and equip the faculty and staff as they changed their vision and direction to that of a problem-based learning environment. Faculty, staff, and Mr. Bates devoted themselves to identifying and communicating their beliefs and the foundations of practice for their school. Every stakeholder joined in creating the best possible learning environment for students. Mr. Bates, faculty, and staff collaboratively developed a school-wide plan to support students in achieving success in the new learning format. The plan provided a structure for creating a physically safe environment as well as an academically secure environment where success was the goal for each student.

When James Johnston became principal of Alice Ott Middle School, there was no mission, strategic plan, or even knowledge of which students were struggling. He collaborated with faculty and staff to develop a mission and plan to overcome the significant achievement gaps among special education, English language, economically disadvantaged, and White students. Their new mission, "To provide a safe, challenging and supportive environment where students are prepared with the fundamentals for success in high school and beyond, developing them into responsible citizens and critical thinkers," and school motto, "Champions find a way!" were truly a collaborative effort reflecting their values and ethics.

Ensuring that Current and Future Practices Are Consistent with the Vision and Mission and Are Based on the Strategic Plan

Strategic thinking involves critically evaluating the school or district in totality to make the best decisions for using limited resources and employing successful practices at all levels (Horwath, 2009). According to Liedtka (1998), strategic thinking also involves *thinking in time*, ensuring that imagined views of the future are not the only driving forces behind the strategy, but identifying gaps between current reality and future intent drives strategic thinking as well.

A leader's ability to maintain high performance expectations buttresses the strategic thinking and enlivens the vision for success. Routinely scheduled data meetings facilitated by leaders support the process of analyzing current practices, the resulting student performance, and the effectiveness of curriculum decisions and instructional practices.

At Alice Ott Middle School, after identifying the mission of the school, they needed to determine how to go about achieving that mission. Principal Johnston printed a list of low achievers and asked teachers to write their own child's name on the list. Johnston then asked, "What would you do if your own child were really on this list?" The answers to that question completely changed their practice. Their main vision became for all students to be on or above grade level in reading by the end of the eighth grade.

Tips for Leaders

- Dedicate a portion of each faculty meeting to reviewing whether specific practices remain consistent with the vision and mission and are based on the strategic plan.
- Survey stakeholders to identify any concerns about consistency of practices.

Administrators, faculty, and staff knew they needed to create significant change. First, they researched successful programs and visited successful schools. Next, they changed the way the schedule worked. They created a planning team that included faculty, parents, and administrators and completed a needs assessment for the school. Finally, they developed a new reading program created to achieve their end-of-the-eighth-grade success vision for all students. The new program included interventions that diagnosed and overcame students' reading difficulties. Every student had an individual plan designed to increase his or her skills. They also instituted a content-area focus on literacy development throughout the school. They created procedures to involve parents and all faculty and staff in the improvement process. Data analysis and input from all stakeholders provided the basis for all of these changes and improvements.

Mr. Johnston was constantly in classrooms. He called it 5/5/5—visiting five classrooms for five minutes five days of the week. Because of this, he was able to see clearly where strengths and weaknesses were. However, he believed that problems were generally due to poor systems rather than to people who were not performing well. Ultimately, Johnston determined that *the systems needed fixing and not the people.*

"Our school is different now," Johnston said. "People believe—students, teachers, parents have confidence. Now we believe that we will make it." And they are making it. Alice Ott was in the top 10% of the schools in the state, an achievement that won them the designation as an Oregon Model School for three years in a row. Alice Ott was named a 2014 MetLife–NASSP Breakthrough School for its academic success and a 2015 Title I Distinguished School for helping low-income students succeed and closing achievement gaps. Principal Johnston received the 2013 Oregon Middle School Principal of the Year award, and Vice Principal Duane Larson was Oregon's 2015 Vice Principal of the year.

Looking Outside the Norm for More Effective Ways of Achieving the Mission, Vision, and Strategic Plan

A willingness to share, to ask, to question their own mental models, and to suggest new and alternative strategies, distinguishes superintendents' and principals' use of strategic thinking from those who embrace practice as usual. Thinking and acting strategically enables effective leaders to communicate and model a clear and focused direction for teaching and learning. Looking for new and innovative ways of achieving the mission, vision, and strategic plan is a hallmark of leaders who make a difference.

Educators often overlook the importance of branding as part of strategic planning for schools and districts. Branding describes why organizations are preeminent and what they deliver that others do not. Leaders need to routinely promote and publicize these qualities as their brand and use them to give everyone, including students, faculty, staff, and stakeholders, a sense of pride and solidarity. This is vital to a vigorous and dynamic learning environment and to a sense of community ownership. Increasingly, training about the school or district brand is crucial.

One example of effective branding is Apple's Genius Bar. The Genius Bar incorporates several qualities of effective brands.

- The brand is humorous, but still comforting.
- The Genius Bar workers are expert and experienced.
- Training is provided with the APPLE method of "**A**pproach customers with a personalized warm welcome, **P**robe to understand the problem, **P**resent a solution, **L**isten for issues, and **E**nd with an invitation to return" (Aaker, 2012).

Tips for Leaders

- Use a how-how diagram (see Appendix A) to identify ways to overcome obstacles to achieving the mission, vision, or strategic plan.
- Use an affinity diagram (see Appendix A) to develop a school or district brand. Include staff, students, and targeted stakeholders.

At Alice Ott, faculty, staff, administrators, and stakeholders constantly investigated ways to achieve the mission, vision, and strategic plan. Collaboration was the norm. There were three school improvement teams—literacy, family involvement, and positive behavioral intervention and support—and every teacher served on one of them. All faculty also participated in subject-area professional learning teams that set goals for student growth, created assessments, and evaluated data-based results.

Mr. Johnston said:

We are all accountable for student success. In addition to the academic measures we have taken to achieve our mission and vision, every teacher contacts at least 10 parents a month with something positive to say about their children. We track these conversations on Google Docs to ensure that all parents are contacted. In addition to the phone calls, we have email weeks and postcard weeks, and we call every student who is absent and go to the home of those who are on our "hot list."

Several principals, to ensure that students grasped the meaning and significance of the mission, asked students in each homeroom to create videos that expressed their perceptions of examples when faculty and staff lived the mission. In addition, they took videos of individual students or small groups of students speaking about their understanding of the meaning of the school's mission.

The Chugach School District (CSD) based their strategic plan on community-wide discussions that began in 1994 about what stakeholders thought graduates should know and be able to do. Strategic planning in CSD followed a continuous improvement cycle.

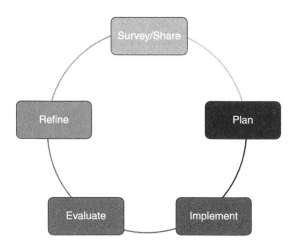

Figure 4.1   Chugach School District Strategic Planning Cycle (from CSD *Strategic News Fall 2014*)

CSD's Strategic Planning Cycle included five strategic focus areas: student focus, staff focus, shared leadership focus, finance and facilities focus, and community and communication focus. Each year, CSD identified goals for the strategic focus areas aligned with their core values of

1. agility,
2. resiliency,
3. valuing stakeholders,
4. performance-based learning,
5. trust and teamwork,
6. continuous improvement and innovation,
7. open and honest communication, and
8. shared leadership and responsibility.

Leading Conversations about the Vision and Mission to Support the Direction of the Organization

Keeping the vision and mission constantly in mind and using them to determine actions in every area are essential for fostering support. Effective leaders model ethical actions and lead conversations to connect the educational community to the larger purpose found in the vision and mission. Stakeholders often respond actively and positively to a vision beyond the obvious in their enthusiasm to connect to a larger purpose.

Student-Led Parent Conferencing was a tool that Principal Faust initiated to develop and enhance communication between students and parents concerning the middle school's vision and mission. At an assigned period in the school day, students shared with parents the nine-week portfolios reflecting their assignments and discussed how their work fulfilled the school's mission. The experience was affirming for students, reinforcing the importance of their work. Faculty observed the conferences during their Collaboration and Professionalism (CAP) time throughout the day and wrote down their reflections on the process. At a later CAP time, faculty debriefed and shared their reflections to improve the process.

Redirecting the focus of Winterboro High School to one of all students' learning at high levels required deliberate faculty-led conversations about mission, vision, teaching, and learning. Principal Bates provided opportunities for faculty to collaborate with their peers and develop strategies to improve instruction in every area. He demonstrated his commitment to supporting faculty by removing or reducing interferences to teaching and providing resources and time to address improved student learning. The dedication of Mr. Bates to the direction of the school; the importance of professional learning for all; maintaining a focus on data; vertical and horizontal collaboration; cross-discipline instruction; and focused, high-level instruction for all students reflected an environment ready to meet any challenge.

Tips for Leaders

- Initiate informal conversations about the vision and mission throughout the day with various people.

- Include the vision and/or mission on every communication with parents and other stakeholders.

- Ensure the deployment of the strategic plan throughout the community.

- Keep the strategic plan in an obvious place where many people will see it. Place a notebook beside it with an invitation to review it and make comments.

Critical Practice 2

Build a Powerful Organization

The design of a powerful organization creates success for everyone. Maria (not her real name) moved to Maplewood Richmond Heights High School from Mexico. She was pregnant and exhibited several behavioral issues that clearly interfered with her learning and success. Principal Kevin Grawer and his 105-Degree Intervention Team included Maria as one of their student participants. Mr. Grawer said:

> I needed to get the trust of Maria's mother, so I began driving Maria home about every two weeks—and then I stayed for dinner. When you sit on someone's couch, drink from their glasses, and eat the tacos they prepared, they know you accept them. Gradually, I became the liaison for Maria's family with daily issues they faced. Maria's mother trusted me; Maria trusted me. And Maria graduated from high school in four years, a result no one would have predicted.

A school or district that is a powerful organization does not allow rules or status quo mindsets to interfere with success for any of its students. Every system and every process support people and facilitate learning for everyone, regardless of age or position. Powerful organizations are strong, effective, energetic, and dynamic, with compelling stories and results. Collaboration and problem solving are pervasive throughout the organization. The organization resolves problems and issues quickly and effectively because the entire organization is agile and flexible and searches for innovative solutions. Superintendents and principals lead faculty, staff, students, and stakeholders in working together to improve processes that increase success and to monitor the effectiveness of processes and procedures.

Working with Others to Create a Powerful Organizational Structure

The driving ethic for any educational institution answers the question, "What is best for students?" Answering this question binds the various elements of the organization into an effective, working model that harnesses the knowledge and emotion of everyone involved. Effective leaders do not attempt to create powerful organizational structures alone. They encourage, support, motivate, and inspire everyone to work together to create a powerful organization that provides the very best for students.

Schools and districts that are powerful organizations provide a sense of order and safety for everyone—students, faculty, and staff. Leaders collaborate with faculty and staff to diagnose the current condition of the organization and to monitor its effectiveness. As you walk through a school that is a powerful organization, you will see faculty and staff in the lounge and the halls, students in classrooms and the cafeteria, parents inside and outside the school all engaging in formal and informal conversations regarding the school environment.

According to *Wayne Richardson*, principal of Deer Valley Elementary School in Hoover, Alabama, the school's leaders made very few school-wide decisions without seeking the opinion of the faculty, usually using Google forms. As faculty shared rationales for their decisions, the leadership team then used this information to craft final decisions. Numerous school-wide decisions—from creating the schedule to structuring professional development time—were made using this process.

Diagnosing the Current Condition of the Organization

Effective diagnosis of an organization's current situation requires collaboration. No one person has all the answers or even knows all the right questions to ask. Administrators, faculty, staff, students, and stakeholders working together, sharing their ideas, thoughts, and beliefs, provide the depth and breadth of analysis necessary for accurate diagnosis.

In 2008, *Denise Ward*, principal of Frank M. Silvia Elementary School in Fall River, Massachusetts, established an instructional leadership team (ILT) and a data team to begin the effort of diagnosing the school's current condition and developing improvement plans. Based on student data, the teams identified strengthening student reading comprehension as a priority need. Faculty focused on school-wide reading comprehension across the curriculum and set student achievement goals. Grade-level teams redesigned planning time and professional learning opportunities to support teaching and learning.

Tips for Leaders

- Develop teams charged with regularly diagnosing school or district issues and making recommendations for solutions.
- Survey stakeholders to obtain their ideas about possible organizational problems.

Faculty posted student data in their classrooms and set up grade-level data boards in the halls to show individual class and school-wide goals and progress. Faculty also established new reading comprehension assessments and rubrics and identified school-wide best practices. They reviewed these best practices regularly during planning and professional learning meetings.

Finally, as they used the new assessments, they diagnosed writing as another student difficulty and expanded the original focus to include helping students communicate more effectively in writing. To support this expanded focus, faculty divided additional learning time into two periods: a literacy period focused on strengthening reading comprehension skills and a writing period focused on improving communication through writing.

Faculty participated in at least two peer observations each year. The peer observations were rich professional development and motivational opportunities for observers and observees.

After leaders, faculty, and staff collaborated to diagnose the current condition of the school and implement changes, students made significant improvement in the annual English/Language Arts (ELA) test at every grade level, and other elementary schools adopted many of Silvia's methods (Kaplan et al., 2014)

The fields of engineering and medicine were the first to advance well-defined, evidence-based models of organizational diagnosis. Following these examples, other professions began developing and implementing their own methods (McFillen et al., 2013). Currently, there are numerous theories of organizational diagnosis used in different fields. In general, though, an effective organizational diagnosis process includes these five steps:

Five-Step Organizational Diagnosis Process

1. Data gathering
2. Analysis
3. Action planning
4. Implementation
5. Evaluation, and revision if necessary

The purpose of organizational diagnosis is to identify disparities between present and desired states and establish the basis for a resolution. Leaders like Denise Ward regularly lead faculty and staff collaboration to identify those gaps and causes. Appendix B, the Five Critical Practices School or District Inventory, and Appendix C, the Five Critical Practices Framework, are effective data gathering tools for organizational diagnosis.

Creating and Securing Order

Successful leaders develop an educational climate that provides a sense of order and safety for engaging others in the teaching and learning processes. Feelings of safety at school positively relate to both academic results and behavioral outcomes (Arum, 2003). In a recent large-scale study of the effect of feelings of safety at school on academic achievement, feeling unsafe exhibited consistent negative effects on test scores (Lacoe, 2013).

Tips for Leaders

- Study the reasons that students with the poorest attendance are not in school or class and make whatever changes are necessary to ensure their learning.
- Use an affinity diagram (see Appendix A) with groups of faculty, staff, students, and stakeholders to identify the areas that they consider disorderly. Then use a cause and effect diagram (see Appendix A) to determine the basic causes of the disorder. Implement solutions for the basic causes.

When *Anael Alston* was appointed principal of Robert M. Finley Middle School in Glen Cove, New York, the superintendent asked him to improve the all-time-low student achievement to prevent state takeover. Dr. Alston decided that his first task was to restore order so that students would be in school and in each class every day. He knew that students who attend school regularly demonstrate higher achievement and higher graduation rates than students who do not attend regularly (Allensworth and Easton, 2005; Romero and Lee, 2007). "Order is not just about kids; it is about teachers and leaders also and how we create a learning environment," Alston said. "We need to develop systems, processes, and protocols to enable professionals to do their best work."

Dr. Alston retained the current faculty and promoted two long-time teachers to assistant principalships. He and his assistant principals then began building relationships by holding programs in churches and community centers and by working with counselors to meet weekly with students who had numerous suspensions for inappropriate behavior. Each student in the group created a plan to guide them throughout middle and high school.

After initially creating order in the school, Alston turned his attention to classroom practices, professional development, and evidence-based supervision. He also led the development of a standardized school-wide study skills system.

Finley was named a 2011 MetLife–NASSP Breakthrough School for its academic success. Also in 2011, the National Association of Secondary School Principals and New York's School Administrators Association designated Dr. Alston the Middle School Principal of the Year. Dr. Alston is the current superintendent of the Hamilton School District.

Engaging Stakeholders in Formal and Informal Conversations Regarding the School or District Environment

> Everyone, ultimately, has a stake in the caliber of schools, and education is everyone's business.
>
> (Fullan, 2011)

There is no doubt that stakeholders will discuss the educational environment. The important question is where and for what purpose? Will stakeholders be talking among themselves, with questionable accuracy, about school and district issues in the school parking lot, grocery store, and ballpark? Or, on the other hand, will these discussions be dialogues with faculty, staff, and administrators with the intention of identifying and resolving problems and celebrating successes? Effective leaders engage stakeholders in both formal and informal conversations about every aspect of the organizational environment.

The Iredell-Statesville School District (I-SS) in Statesville, North Carolina, led by Superintendent *Brady Johnson*, engaged stakeholders in informal conversations about the school environment and continually conducted formal stakeholder surveys. School and district information was shared through Connect-Ed, and schools also used websites and newsletters to share significant information. In order to keep stakeholders knowledgeable about district goals and achievement and to let them respond about district issues, the district regularly circulated a newsletter that provided for community feedback. E-news items about district celebrations, goals, and other information regularly informed subscribing parents.

Tips for Leaders

- Identify and use numerous, varied methods to engage stakeholders in discussions about the school or district.

- Increase communication with families and other stakeholders. Set a target goal for the number and type of communications each week. Identify persons responsible for each type of communication.

- There are numerous ideas for communication methods with stakeholders, including letters of introduction, orientation meetings, information notes, telephone conferences, emails, photographs of school or district activities, social media, and thank you notes.

Each year I-SS distributed stakeholder satisfaction surveys to all students, faculty, and staff members, random samples of parents, and certain stakeholders. Data obtained from these surveys informed program and process improvements in the district and schools. I-SS leaders regularly celebrated successes and identified opportunities for improvement, then used this information to improve key processes (BNQP, 2008). As a result of its numerous improvements, I-SS won the 2008 Baldridge National Quality Award.

Collaborating with Stakeholders to Monitor the Effectiveness of Processes and Procedures

Including all stakeholders in determining process effectiveness supports the goal of improved student learning and maintains the visibility of the work of the educational community to meet that goal. Superintendents and principals cannot lead the work and maintain the focus of the direction alone. Engaging others is key to developing a powerful organization.

According to Superintendent *JoAnn Sternke*, everyone in the Pewaukee School District (PSD) in Pewaukee, Wisconsin, focused on four critical areas: people, planning, results, and process improvement. They continuously reviewed and assessed customer requirements and what engaged employees. Frequent monitoring of how they were delivering on their key responsibilities ensured effectiveness and created student, employee, and stakeholder loyalty. Dr. Sternke said:

Our work is a work of the heart. Everyone collaborates to create the action plan so <u>everyone</u>—including teachers, custodians, bus drivers, and cafeteria workers—understands their role in helping students learn. We all have pride in our mission and a role in accomplishing this "work of the heart." We have linked our work of the heart to our strategic plan, and about 70 stakeholders are included in developing annual strategic plans. We display our results in a balanced scorecard so that people understand how well we are doing and where we need to improve. Involving internal and external stakeholders has helped in improving system effectiveness in all areas.

Tips for Leaders

- Include significant numbers of stakeholders in the development and review of processes and procedures.

- Gather stories of success and share liberally with the community so stakeholders know about processes that are effective.

- Involve the community in improvement efforts.

- Create a process (*with a required response time*) to ensure a quick and effective resolution of problems and issues.

PSD employed many different stakeholder listening approaches to gathering information designed to improve processes and procedures. They used a wide variety of print and technology tools depending on stakeholder needs. For example, they used annual parent, employee, and student satisfaction surveys as their key tool to obtain what they call "Voice of Customer" data. The survey covered satisfaction and dissatisfaction data concerning engagement, service, safety, communication, and quality. Teams identified district trends and, if appropriate, integrated opportunities for improvement into action plans.

A priority at PSD was to *exceed expectations* in relationships with stakeholders through frequent and regular communications. PSD used a six-step Concern/Suggestion Tracking System that provided a deep understanding of stakeholder problems and tracked resolutions. All staff responded to incoming complaints within 24 hours, with a status update or resolution provided within seven workdays.

PSD results were substantial. In addition to student achievement increases, advanced placement offerings increased, and graduates attending postsecondary education increased. PSD won the prestigious 2013 Baldrige National Quality Award. In 2013, according to *Newsweek* magazine, Pewaukee High ranked in the top 6% of the nation's high schools. The *Washington Post* named it one of the most challenging high schools in the nation, and Dr. Sternke received recognition as the 2013 Wisconsin Superintendent of the Year.

Leading an Organization in Becoming Agile and Flexible

High-performance organizations are agile and flexible. They are able to respond rapidly and effectively to changes in student needs, stakeholder requirements, and the necessities of the global economy. These schools and districts handle complexity easily because they bring together the ideas, wisdom, and heart of everyone involved. Leaders of agile organizations make sure that everyone is involved in reflecting, examining solutions to problems, participating in sincere conversations, and looking for out-of-the-box resolutions to problems.

> Leading in a culture of change means creating a culture (not just a structure) of change. It does not mean adopting innovations, one after another; it does mean producing the capacity to see, critically assess, and selectively incorporate new ideas and practices—all the time, inside the organization as well as outside it.
>
> (Fullan, 2001, p. 79)

Engaging Others in Reflective Processes

Effective faculty critically examine their teaching, and effective leaders constantly consider their effectiveness and model reflective processes. The best reflection that creates agility and flexibility in an organization occurs not in isolation, but with others. Reflection, which includes listening, responding, debating, discussing, and collaborating, can also include analyzing a previous experience or questioning a current practice. Reflection is central to learning and innovation, providing the basis for making useful changes, maintaining efforts that are successful, and building on or adapting past information based on the latest knowledge and best practices. Leaders can help faculty improve their reflection skills by leading discussions about difficult issues, demonstrating active listening, and responding to concerns.

Tips for Leaders

- Create common workspaces to encourage candid dialogue and collaboration. Consider developing a "team room."
- Ensure that teams include members from different areas and with different responsibilities.

Listening and responding are powerful tools for leaders to initiate and support growth and change within a school or district. Listening and responding are encouraging and validating, declaring for the listener, "You are important, and your ideas matter." Listening and responding are reassuring and inspiring; they say for the listener, "I know what is important to you, and I believe you can achieve your goals." Effective leaders listen and respond in order to encourage, validate, reassure, and inspire others and to involve others in reflecting.

Listening and responding also support growth, trust, and student learning. Leana and her co-workers studied more than 1,200 teachers and found that "students showed higher gains in math achievement when their teachers reported frequent conversations with their peers that centered on math and when there was a feeling of trust or closeness among teachers" (Leana, 2011, p. 33).

Pewaukee School District leaders and faculty used many varied methods to listen to students and other stakeholders and engage them in reflection, including student, parent, and community focus groups, conferences, a website suggestion box, and Board of Education meetings.

Creating Risk-Free Opportunities to Develop Solutions to Problems

An effective leader creates an environment that gives faculty, staff, and students the freedom to take risks, which provides opportunities for problem solving in ways that might not be routine or familiar. A primary commitment of effective leaders is to create the environment and many opportunities for faculty, staff, and students to implement innovative strategies and courses of action. Evaluating, without censure, the effectiveness of these strategies is a critical part of determining the best practices for deepening the learning for each student.

Tips for Leaders

- Look beyond education to find best practices. Subscribe to business, health care, and non-profit magazines or journals that are focused on problem solving and innovation. Position them in a place of prominence so others will see and read them.
- When identifying a goal or a problem, make sure that flexibility is part of the result or solution. Ask people who make requests for a new resource or program if it will support flexibility.
- Recognize and celebrate solutions, even those that do not work.

All Maplewood Richmond Heights faculty participated in risk-free working teams. The teams, which included an intervention team, a literacy team, a professional development team, a building advisory team, a teaching and learning committee that also included parents, and an honors committee, examined solutions to problems and performed the organizational work of the school.

The 105-Degree Fever team dedicated itself to helping students who were in need of significant intervention to create success in their lives. Each member of the team carried a small caseload, not more than eight students, and completed all interventions during school hours.

The 105-Degree Protocol ensured adequate interventions for each student and called for team members to implement four critical actions for all students identified by the teams.

105-Degree Protocol

1. The team member calls and visits each student's home to develop a relationship with the parent and student.

2. The team member meets with the student at least once a week.

3. The team member updates the 105-Degree Fever team.

4. The team member updates the student's data points on the Universal Screener chart, which includes achievement results, grades, and attendance, at least every three weeks.

In addition to following the protocol for every 105-degree student, Principal Grawer and the team did *whatever it took to make changes to ensure student growth and success*. Mr. Grawer said:

> We always say, "One size fits each, and we have to find the each."
> I will change a student's schedule any time it is necessary. I may
> have a student attend four or five classes and several guided study
> halls. These guided study halls include no more than five to seven
> students and are led by excellent teachers. What we are doing is
> maximizing everything to give these students what they need.

Kevin Grawer received recognition as a Walsworth Consummate Professional in 2012. Student achievement and ACT averages showed significant increases, and Maplewood Richmond Heights High School was named a 2013 MetLife–NASSP Breakthrough School for its academic success.

Principal Bates constantly and consistently asked Winterboro parents, students, faculty, and staff, "What are you going to accomplish today? What can we do to help you?" He used these questions to create a dynamic that continuously engaged others in thinking about and examining solutions to problems.

Encouraging Open and Professional Dialogue to Confront Obstacles That Stall Progress

Numerous internal barriers can slow progress in an organization. A lack of open communication is one of those difficulties that weakens success and halts improvement. Frank and honest communication builds strong relationships, understanding, respect, and trust and enables colleagues to work together to create positive change.

Several leaders used the *looking at student work protocol* to encourage open and professional dialogue. This effort to analyze and improve student work often began when faculty realized that some of their lessons did not grab the attention or interest of the students, and therefore little learning occurred. Including students in discussions of lessons validated the students' ideas and clearly communicated that the school existed to deepen their learning. Students' concrete feedback about their work provided faculty with invaluable information and guided revisions in class structure and lessons.

Tips for Leaders

- Develop methods for *listening to and learning from* stakeholders about obstacles. Surveys, focus groups, roundtables, and advisory committees are some examples.
- Conduct stakeholder program reviews. Ask: "what is working, what is not working, and how can we improve the program?"
- Identify and implement methods for listening to student voice.
- Consider implementing *Looking at student work* (http://www.lasw.org/index.html).

Operating on a generally random basis, faculty selected student focus group participants to gather their input on how they learn and the work provided them. Students then followed a protocol to give their perceptions of previously provided assignments and the learning that occurred from the assignments. When students completed their discussions, faculty followed another protocol to ask students clarifying questions and probe for strategies to improve the learning. Faculty often observed that as students participated in this open dialogue, their interest and connection to learning increased and they were inspired to pursue independent learning. After completion of the process, students usually acknowledged a new appreciation for the hard work of faculty when creating lessons.

Principal Tomlinson led open dialogue meetings designed to recognize and remove barriers to student achievement. Faculty met regularly in communities of practice and addressed topics identified by leaders, faculty, staff, and stakeholders. They regularly reviewed programs and constantly communicated with each other and with students and their families about student progress.

George Hall faculty and staff worked constantly to identify obstacles that stalled progress and to find solutions. They shared best practices and celebrated successes. The team room, a common workspace, was used almost every day and encouraged open dialogue, helped build collaboration, and decreased faculty isolation.

At Winston Campus Elementary School in Palatine, Illinois, Principal *Andy Tieman* believed that "continuous systemic improvements take time. Before change can happen, you have to confront the road blocks." He found that "the best way to do this is to have open and professional conversations with the stakeholders who are involved." Tieman further explained:

> I always prepare myself with data or evidence to support the improvement efforts. You have to assess where you are currently and support the change process with meaningful data. Your conversations move away from personal agendas to what is best for kids and for your school. When using data, you can identify root causes and have conversations about improvement efforts. Getting everyone on the same page is not easy, but when you confront the obstacles and support your efforts with data, the process becomes much easier and change can happen.

Engaging Stakeholders in Discussions for Out-of-the-Box Answers to Difficult Problems

Effective leaders engage in breakthrough thinking, often "outside the building" thinking. They use ideas from diverse fields, finding the intersections between different ideas and using these connections to engage the collective brainpower of the organization in searching for best practices. They provide support and encouragement for faculty and staff innovations, especially student-focused innovations. According to George Hall's Principal Tomlinson, "I believe that when children are involved, it is not a question of thinking outside the box—there really is no box."

Tips for Leaders

- Create a process that requires looking beyond typical methods when addressing issues.
- Recognize and celebrate new ways to solve problems.
- Talk about, encourage, recognize, and reward swift and responsive solutions to problems.
- Include stakeholders on teams and committees that are problem-solving difficult issues.

The Chugach School District (CSD), on the basis of stakeholder input, developed a shared purpose, a five-year timeline of activities, and one-year targets. They identified and prioritized goals and developed and implemented action plans. The goals were their Five Focus Areas: Basic Skills, Individual Needs of Students, Technology, Transition (School to Life), and Character Development.

In addition, using stakeholder input, CSD developed an entirely new way of organizing school. CSD delivered instruction from preschool up to age 21, 24 hours a day, seven days a week—in the work place, in the community, in the home, and in school.

There were no grade levels; instead, students carried around individual progress report packets that outlined their progress through the district's learning standards. Students now had a clear road map to help them navigate from where they were currently performing to where they would perform at graduation levels. Students all knew exactly where they were as they moved through the standards. They knew if they were at level seven in math or level six in reading. Students kept track of how far they had progressed, using markers and multicolored highlighters. To move to the next level, each student learned every subject at every level, passing with at least 80% proficiency. In addition, they graduated whenever they mastered all of the standards, not when they reached an arbitrary age.

At Deer Valley Elementary School, Dr. Richardson typically shared scenarios in faculty meetings to develop out-of-the-box possibilities. Faculty sat together in vertical and cross-functional teams, comprised of a teacher from each grade level, a "specials" teacher, and a special education teacher. Teams ensured a focus on developing positive and innovative solutions to problems.

While it is important to accomplish the essential important tasks of running the school or the district, it is also critical to remember that the "coexistence of creative behavior and an execution culture—getting things done—requires careful managing. It's too easy for the execution culture to kill the creative culture" (Merrill, 2015, p. 44). When leaders of high-performing schools and districts engage stakeholders in conversations about looking for new answers to difficult problems, they reinforce organizational agility and flexibility.

Leading Others in Developing, Maintaining, and Improving Processes That Increase the Effectiveness of the Organization

Leaders of high-performing schools and districts ensure continuous improvement of programs, processes, and performance. They involve stakeholders in systematic and focused analyses of processes and procedures in order to accurately measure effectiveness and efficiency in areas of most importance. They identify areas that matter most and accurately measure improvement. Leaders support mid-course improvements and collaborate with faculty and staff on next steps to meet difficult objectives that will improve student learning and satisfy stakeholders.

Engaging Stakeholders in Discussions of Performance Effectiveness in All Areas

Performance improvements in schools and districts encompass all areas, including curriculum, instruction, building cleanliness, food services, transportation, and many others. Discussions about program effectiveness that include only a special few are often less successful, and much less productive, than those discussions that are more inclusive. Leaders will ensure success as they work toward creating successful organizations when they engage many stakeholders at various times and in diverse places.

At Deer Valley Elementary School, Principal Richardson talked to parents, students, and faculty throughout the day, always reflecting on the mission statement and performance effectiveness. Through this process, he identified faculty to present at the school's Inspire sessions, which were set up like Ted talks. Dr. Richardson said:

> Teachers share things that they have done in their classroom (or things that they would like to do in their classroom) in which students have been inspired to take initiative in their own learning. This has had a positive effect on the facilitation of ideas and programs between the classrooms.

Listening to student voice is a powerful example of engaging stakeholders in discussions to bring about quality improvement. Students can serve as information sources, collaborators in action research, and co-designers of school improvement efforts. When students function as equal collaborators in improvement efforts, there is the highest potential for impact on school success (Lee and Zimmerman, n.d.; Raymond, 2001).

Identify Areas that Matter Most and Are Worth Measuring

Conversations about schools and schooling take place everywhere, but are many times about topics that make little difference in the areas identified as most important. Leaders of high-performing organizations encourage, support, and lead conversations that recognize what matters most and what is worth measuring. Leaders also ensure that the areas that matter most are measured and evaluated for continuous improvement. As a strategy point, what matters most to an organization should be discernible from its mission and vision.

Tips for Leaders

- Start by identifying what faculty, staff, students, and stakeholders think is most important. Chugach School District is an excellent example of this.
- Surveys and focus groups are two methods that work well. In the focus groups, affinity diagrams (see Appendix A) gather opinions and thoughts quickly and accurately.
- Develop a protocol for identifying the areas that are most important.

In the Iredell-Statesville School District, faculty made decisions that affected curriculum, instruction, and assessment. They reviewed and used data to make decisions about student learning, finance, maintenance, and personnel issues. Leaders facilitated conversations with everyone about the district's vision, mission, and values, and questioned participants on strategies to support student learning (BNQP, 2008).

Deer Valley Elementary School faculty began the revision of their mission statement by setting up a graffiti board with the following question at the top: "What do we want our students to be when they leave the 12th grade?" The wording of this question was critical because it focused not on what faculty wanted students to know or be able to do but instead on the more basic WHO they wanted students to be. Faculty then began identifying and reviewing the covenants they made to their students, parents, and each other. According to Dr. Richardson, "The combination of these two processes provided the direction that is currently leading the decisions of the leadership team."

Engaging Others in Accurately Measuring Improvement in Areas of Most Importance

Tips for Leaders

- Develop systematic, straightforward processes for gathering information that everyone understands.

- Regularly evaluate the information-gathering processes for effectiveness.

- Make sure the information-gathering processes are necessary and that the results will provide information that staff actually use.

- Identify and use specific tools, such as the PDSA, that staff, students, and stakeholders understand.

Many processes and actions are measurable. However, not all items that are measured are of equal importance. Clearly, some issues matter more than others when the consideration is student learning and safety. Leaders guide others in a systematic analysis of what is most important by collaboratively identifying and developing effective measures.

Numerous and varied processes and tools are available for measuring improvement. However, the random use of such tools, without identifying the areas of greatest importance in creating improvement and growth, only serves to expend time and effort without ensuring success. In today's fast-paced education environment, no one has the extra time and effort to devote to work that has a minimal chance of success. In addition, educators often unsuccessfully use the measurement tools of the past to assess and report the new learning simply because they are comfortable with those tools. Leaders of high-performing organizations engage others in identifying the areas of most consequence and using appropriate tools to measure improvement in those areas.

At Frank M. Silvia Elementary School, discussions about measuring improvement are not limited to data meetings. Faculty discuss goals and assessment results with students. In addition, faculty post in the hallways each student's goals and progress, identified only by a number. In this way, students are able to monitor their individual performance and view the results of their class (Kaplan et al., 2014).

Leading Others in Making Mid-course Adjustments for Improvement

Leaders of high-performing schools and districts model ways to make mid-course corrections to ensure student success. Leaders set aside time to work with faculty in identifying the mid-course changes that will make a difference for students.

Tips for Leaders

- Provide the data needed to make effective mid-course adjustments.
- Use a PDSA process (see p. 91) to identify and implement mid-course adjustments.
- Include student voice as a data point for making mid-course adjustments.
- Recognize and celebrate staff who make mid-course adjustments for improvement.

Winston Campus faculty used a Plan–Do–Study–Act (PDSA) process to support school improvement plans and make necessary mid-course adjustments in individual classrooms and throughout the school. In 2007, in order to increase writing achievement, Principal Tieman led a two-year PDSA improvement effort. He and his team used PDSAs to co-ordinate, facilitate, and monitor their improvement efforts. As a result, the percentage of sixth-grade students meeting or exceeding state writing standards increased from 59% to 95%. Winston received a 2008 Academic Excellence Award on the Illinois Honor Roll, a list of high-achieving schools in Illinois.

At George Hall Elementary School, faculty used PDSAs to support school improvement plans and make needed mid-course adjustments. PDSA charts lined the walls of the team room and were used to advance success in almost every area. Principal Tomlinson and George Hall faculty used PDSAs to improve instruction, inclusion plans, parental involvement, transitional plans, and interdisciplinary strategies.

Critical Practice 3

Ensure Student-Focused Vision and Action

Leaders who guide organizations in identifying and maintaining the beliefs and values of that organization establish the focus and direction of the work. Effective leaders develop stakeholders' understanding of creating environments that focus on student learning. They create a student-centered vision and culture, provide instructional leadership, and lead the development of guidelines and procedures for learning.

Creating a Vision and Culture That Focus on Student Learning and Student Needs

Ensuring that a school's or district's vision and actions are student-focused prioritizes efforts so that faculty, staff, and students have the necessary resources for success, and the learning opportunities for students to improve continuously. Leaders of high-performing organizations include stakeholders in crafting the vision and ensure that processes support student learning.

Leading Stakeholders in Crafting a Student-Centered Vision

Many schools or districts develop vision statements that focus on student needs. Often, however, the actions that occur within the organization do not reflect the vision. The dissonance between stated visions and day-to-day actions usually reflects a lack of commitment to common beliefs, which results in "lip service" to the vision and mission. Students and parents quickly observe a lack of coherence and lose faith and trust in the school or district.

Tips for Leaders

Facilitate conversations with staff, identifying their core beliefs about teaching and learning. Determine the non-negotiables, the go-to-the-mat beliefs about learning. Use an affinity diagram (see Appendix A) to identify non-negotiables.

Forging a common set of student-focused beliefs requires a willingness of stakeholders to reflect honestly on sometimes long-held stated and unstated ideas about students and learning. Effective leaders prepare internal and external stakeholders for anticipated changes in "how we do school." Through formal and informal conversations, leaders build stakeholders' understanding of the demands of the evolving global society and the skills required for students to succeed in the future. As superintendents and principals lead educators in collaboratively identifying their core beliefs about learning, student focus, and the role of faculty, a blueprint of the culture emerges, and the tone and expectations are established. Leaders of high-performing schools and districts actively lead faculty and staff in the process of basing decisions and actions on student-focused visions, avoiding the pitfall of "trying on for size" or actually adopting each new program, strategy, or "magic bullet" in the current literature. Principals and superintendents in these studies led their staffs in journeys of reflection and self-evaluation, taking them from business as usual to cultures that embraced visions and actions focused on student learning and student needs.

At Kennedy Elementary School in Norman, Oklahoma, Principal *Montie Koehn* took every opportunity to interject guiding questions into conversations with faculty that caused them to think deeply about their personal beliefs concerning student learning and their roles in leading the learning. Faculty identified numerous principles or beliefs that guided their work with students. Ms. Koehn facilitated the faculty's work of narrowing the statements to the non-negotiable beliefs that provided the direction for Kennedy's student-centered vision.

Leaders Koehn, Tomlinson, and Freeman shared a benefit of hiring all new faculty when assuming their roles as principals and superintendent. Their unique situations allowed the three leaders to select faculty who embraced the direction of a student-focused vision. Examining every initiative, emphasis, or new practice through the lens of vision and mission provided concrete support for these leaders and enabled them to maintain the direction of the schools. As parents, faculty, or students proposed new practices or initiatives about teaching and learning, these effective leaders guided them through a process of reaffirming their beliefs and determining if the new practices or initiatives mirrored the beliefs of the school or district.

Ensuring that Learning Is the Focus of Student Work

Faculty sharing time is an absolute to achieve the goal of student-focused work.

As leaders provide protected and focused time for faculty to engage in professional dialogue, faculty learn and refine new skills and collectively develop strategies for the implementation of difficult or new content. Following the implementation of the new skills, faculty return to the collaborative time and, with their colleagues, examine their execution of the lessons and the outcomes of student performance when meeting the content standards. These conversations afford faculty the opportunity to share their successes and seek guidance or redirection from peers without fear of retribution or embarrassment. As faculty experience the safe and judgment-free environment of mutual sharing and collaboration with colleagues, their knowledge and willingness to persist in creating high-level work for students increase, and faculty and student confidence grows.

Tips for Leaders

- Adhere to school norms for student and faculty behaviors to foster a safe environment for learning during collaboration time, discussions, focus groups, and other interactive experiences.
- Establish and protect from interruption a daily, embedded time for faculty collaboration, and ensure the focus of the time is enhancing teaching practice.

The actions and emphases of these effective leaders maintained a focus on student learning and provided a clear message to all stakeholders. Professional dialogue among faculty, staff, and principals encouraged reinforcement of the priorities of the schools and districts and gave voice to their commitment to creating high-quality work for their students.

Pewaukee School District's mission is: "Through our unique all-school campus setting, the Pewaukee Public School District will open the door to each child's future. Our School Community delivers an innovative and progressive education" (Pewaukee School District, 2015). The execution of this mission generates a vital and dynamic approach to student learning. Faculty use benchmarks, leading indicators, and data to adapt their teaching methods to meet the individual needs of every student. Leaders and faculty collaborate to implement individualized learning using a district-wide, locally designed curriculum and curriculum design and review process.

Facilitating the Development of Processes that Support Student Learning

Tips for Leaders

- Develop teachers' and students' skills of reflective thinking about their teaching and learning. Lead students to reflect on strategies for problem solving.
- Through focus groups, guide faculty in gathering the voices of students concerning the quality of their learning experiences. Use the opportunities to identify how students learn best.

Leaders in these case studies designed processes focusing on the students and their learning rather than on the adults in the school. Focusing on student learning did not indicate that adults were unimportant or not valued, quite the contrary. The adults created the stimulating environment and developed opportunities that fostered the focus on student learning. For many adults, the schools of the past concentrated on fitting students into a particular mold or ideal. If students did not fit the teacher's ideal, they failed. The processes of schools of the past emphasized the role of the teacher as primary and students as secondary. Innovative, successful superintendents and principals of today guide their staffs in designing the kind of experiences where faculty and students work as collaborators and co-learners. Leaders in these case studies also provided specific guidelines and procedures for student-focused instruction. Leadership teams, faculty, and staff developed or reviewed practices that ensured the schools and districts remained student-focused.

These effective leaders created environments that supported faculty in providing students with authentic experiences and led students to reflect on their learning. Several of the leaders contended that reflective thinking was not a skill students (and sometimes faculty) typically possessed. Faculty developed strategies and prompts that guided students in thinking about their learning when solving complex problems. A seventh grade teacher described teacher-created situations that provided students with opportunities to "step back and think about how they actually solved the problems." As students talked through steps to solve problems, they grasped the concept that problem solving involved specific steps that were transferable to other situations in school as well as in life. The practice of guiding students through the process enabled them to develop the skill of reflecting on their own learning.

Effective leaders in these schools and districts identified strategies and procedures that ensured the overarching direction of each school was increased student learning. A few of the practices of these effective principals included the following:

- gathering student voice through focus groups, surveys, or one-on-one conversations;
- analyzing student work as a team;
- scrutinizing and reworking lessons that do not result in learning at high levels;
- highlighting student successes;
- including student and parent input and participation in the work of the leadership team;
- providing immediate and additional academic support for students struggling with concepts;
- creating and protecting a safe learning environment for all—students, faculty, and staff;
- communicating the value of the work of all students.

The implementation of focus groups created an environment that validated stakeholders by actively pursuing the voices of faculty, staff, students, and parents about how students learn best. The practice grew as a tool for determining perceived strengths and weaknesses in the instructional program and generating possible solutions or next steps. As students participated in focus groups, they realized that faculty genuinely wanted their input about how they learned (learning styles), instructional strategies that were most meaningful for their learning, and suggestions for increasing their interest in the content (engagement). Faculty guided students in thinking more deeply about their learning, and students grew in ownership and understanding of their responsibilities in learning.

Leading Faculty and Staff in Maintaining a Focus on Student Learning

> Ultimately, the critical factors to effecting changes in student learning are the changes in instructional practice that occur daily, teacher by teacher, in every area.

Effective leaders realize that maintaining a focus on student learning requires consistent and genuine support for faculty and staff. Leaders understand and give voice to the fact that faculty are willing and able to expend their energy improving their practice so that students benefit and thrive in the changing world. Conversations among colleagues, observations of peer teachers' instructional practices, and participation in lesson studies afford faculty opportunities to expand their skills.

Leaders realize that educator practice will not change until everyone wholly acknowledges and commits to personal accountability and responsibility for improved instruction. A roadblock to cultural change is the difficult recognition that some valued, past practices no longer meet the needs of today's students. A compelling role for effective leaders is to develop and sustain climates of *learning for all*, students and adults, within the education community. *Learning for all includes "letting go" of long-treasured units of study or teaching practices that no longer meet the needs of students and replacing them with best practices for today's students.*

Case study leaders recognized that collaboration built security and trust among faculty and staff to step out of their comfort zones and risk new strategies. Leaders' encouragement of faculty innovation and the belief in *a risk-free environment* (Schlechty, 2002) supported a shift from a focus on teaching to a focus on learning.

Tips for Leaders

- Maintain a commitment with faculty and staff to providing high-quality learning experiences for students. Lead faculty and staff in letting go of long-held "sacred cow" units of study that no longer meet the needs of students. Use an affinity diagram (see Appendix A) to identify the types of new units that will meet the students' needs.

- Lead faculty in analyzing samples of student work for clarity of the assignments and in assessing students' mastery of the content.

- When anyone requests a new program or resource, ask for a description of how it will enhance student learning and how it supports the vision for the school or district.

Faculty and staff support presents itself in a variety of formats. Instructional peer coaching is one format for faculty support. Leaders share and encourage faculty self-reflection and mutual peer reflection through instructional peer coaching. Principals indicate that peer coaching provides a non-evaluative format for colleagues to share materials and ideas and collaborate on creating lessons for the most difficult to teach concepts. Everyone benefits from the combined knowledge of the faculty to enhance their learning. Unexpected, and sometimes unintended, outcomes of instructional peer coaching include a decreased sense of faculty isolation and an increased culture of cooperation and support among professional colleagues.

Principal Bates' support for the weekly Friday Teacher Academy provided Winterboro faculty with the necessary time to analyze student performance and identify those students failing to master specific skills. As faculty posted visuals of student work samples and composites of student data in the Teacher Academy room, they analyzed the effectiveness of their instructional practices, collaborated on next steps, and coached one another to refine or improve those practices. Faculty also created cross-content lessons during Teacher Academy that integrated two or more disciplines into one collaborative unit with a final culminating event or product that solved a previously identified problem. According to Mr. Bates, the benefits of project-based learning were many, but the authenticity of the units in concert with students' opportunities to conduct inquiry brought real life experiences into the school. The experience of learning through inquiry developed students' thinking and investigation skills and prepared them for solving life problems and issues in the future.

A key emphasis for Principal *Amy Swann* and the faculty of Bate Middle School in Danville, Kentucky, was not only to increase their skills and capacity to teach the content, but also to equip students with necessary skills required for success throughout their lives. Listening to students' voices about their learning and ways they learned best, while addressing the needs of the whole child, enabled Bate Middle School faculty to focus clearly on students and their learning. Implementation of project-based learning environments at Bate Middle School and at Winterboro High School enabled students to develop necessary 21st century skills. These skills included the use of technology, critical thinking, reflecting on their contributions to a group, collaboration, communication, problem solving, team building, time management, and presentation skills. Principals Bates and Swann maintained their schools' focus on students' mastery of the required content, while simultaneously developing reflective thinking practices and critical skills necessary for success.

Providing Instructional Leadership

Effective leaders consistently demonstrate the skills necessary to guide internal and external stakeholders to reach desired outcomes. Leaders anticipate interruptions or detours in the change process, monitor progress, and communicate and redirect discrepancies between desired outcomes and reality. They coordinate experiences that enhance learning, establish a culture of mutual respect, lead conversations about learning experiences, and ensure improvement in teaching practices.

Coordinating Faculty and Staff Experiences That Enhance Learning for All

Tips for Leaders

- Email solid research articles relevant to your faculty and staff, and ask them to read and respond at the next team meeting. Assist faculty and staff in implementing newly acquired strategies and sharing outcomes with their collaborative groups. Follow a lesson study protocol to guide the process in a non-threatening manner. (For a guide to lesson study, see http://www.tc.columbia.edu/lessonstudy/tools.html.)

- Emphasize to stakeholders the culture of learning for all. Provide professional learning opportunities for faculty and staff.

Support from grants and state and national recognitions enabled Kennedy Elementary to continue their emphases on research-based professional learning. As part of the culture of Kennedy, Principal Koehn and faculty routinely examined the effectiveness of their instructional practices and identified possible changes that could result in improved student learning. Ms. Koehn deliberately nurtured a school culture of learning for all. The learning culture came to life when faculty participated in "Intentional Planning," a workshop model of professional learning. Faculty colleagues volunteered to present sessions for their peers reflecting best practices in a particular strategy or content. Participants received an advance listing of learning options from which to choose, and made their selections. Faculty facilitators led the sessions and shared new learning with participants. Participants then implemented the newly learned practices in their classrooms and returned to the next session of "Intentional Planning" to share their reflections about the implementation. Faculty feedback, kudos, and suggestions for next steps guided their colleagues in refining or reworking their lessons and practice. The cycle of learning, implementation, reflection, and refining continued throughout each academic year.

Ms. Koehn also provided release time for faculty to observe their peers. She guided faculty to observe other faculty with strengths that the observer did not possess. Ms. Koehn provided each observer with a reflection template and a list of "look fors" to complete while in the classroom. Ms. Koehn reflected with faculty on the experience later and discussed positive "take-aways" from the observation.

> Strong leaders provide faculty with needed resources and protect their time to expand their collective knowledge and application of best teaching practices.

Dr. Swann lived her belief that as a professional educator her moral obligation was to provide continuous, meaningful, and deliberate professional learning experiences for all faculty and staff, including herself. Other case study leaders encouraged routine professional discourse among faculty, staff, and community, demonstrating respect for all stakeholders' varying opinions while discussing the positive value of incorporating new strategies or information into teaching methods.

Effective leaders learn continuously but have no misconception that they are the only "holders of the knowledge." As members of a professional learning community, successful leaders encourage internal and external training that deepens faculty and staff commitment to instruction that enhances student learning.

Facilitating Conversations Regarding Challenging, Attainable Learning Experiences

Tips for Leaders

- Establish PLCs to address specific learning needs for faculty and staff. Monitor the effectiveness and leadership within the PLCs. Redirect the work of the team, if necessary.

- Oversee the work of PLCs to ensure a positive focus and encouraging influence.

- Underline the critical importance of maintaining a safe, risk-free environment for faculty and staff. Remind teams of the vulnerability of sharing their experiences. Emphasize that *what happens in team time stays in team time.*

- Lead faculty in developing or sharing strategies for differentiating instruction to meet the various ability and skill levels of students. Ensure the implementation of the strategies.

The forward thinking leaders in these case studies encouraged professional reading in support of research-based instructional strategies to guide professional learning. As faculty participated in prior professional development and training in instructional emphases, they led their peers in deepening their growth and knowledge through book studies, Intentional Planning, PAC (practicing active character), Friday Teacher Academies, and other PLCs (professional learning communities). PLCs organized themselves according to grade levels, instructional interests, or content areas. Leaders established the clear expectation that conversations in PLCs focused on the important work of faculty creating the best possible lessons and learning environments for the work of students. Previously established cultures of learning and professional growth supported faculty presenters as they shared with their peers. The PLCs reinforced conversations about the new learning and served as a lifeline for faculty while implementing new practices. As faculty applied new strategies and discussed the performance of students with their colleagues, their fears of consequences for failures lessened. The professional dialogue and encouragement from peers reassured faculty that they were supported in the process of growing and stretching themselves as professionals.

Leaders of effective schools and districts guide faculty in exploring possibilities for differentiating lessons to meet the variety of student learning needs. Effective leaders engage faculty in candid conversations, often focusing on differentiated instructional strategies, student learning styles, and adaptations or modifications of lessons to address divergent learning abilities and meet the needs of all students. The very act of leading these discussions demonstrates the leader's strong sense of commitment and obligation to providing challenging, yet attainable, learning opportunities for students at all levels of ability.

Modeling and Encouraging Mutual Respect among Stakeholders

Ms. Koehn led faculty and staff in creating a supportive learning environment at Kennedy Elementary School through the establishment of a culture of mutual respect among the adults and students. Koehn, faculty, and staff identified specific expectations for all stakeholders in support of the work of the school. The expectations reinforced the school culture and direction and provided a model of life skills so that students learned to live within the community. To underscore the culture, students set goals and standards of excellence for themselves and their peers. Faculty and staff emphasized the expectations by upholding high standards for themselves and supporting colleagues in their quest for quality work. Students embraced the expectations and readily recited them as an indication of their belief in the power of the message.

Koehn related an example of deepening the culture of respect in the school community. A group of fifth-grade boys continually disrupted the learning process in their individual classrooms. Numerous disciplinary trips to the principal's office made no difference in the behaviors. Ms. Koehn

Tips for Leaders

Review routinely the commitment to respect among faculty, staff, students, and other stakeholders.

collected anecdotal data from each of the teachers to determine any commonality among the behaviors. Koehn and the faculty analyzed the data and found one common factor in each of the boys' lives. The boys' fathers no longer lived in their homes. Incarceration of the fathers left the boys no day-to-day male influence in their lives. Koehn and the faculty recruited male community volunteers who agreed to mentor the boys weekly for a year. The mentors modeled respect for the boys, reinforced their academic successes, supported and tutored them in their failures, and encouraged them in developing the social skills necessary for success. Over time, the behaviors and academic performance of the boys improved markedly. Self-confidence and self-respect replaced self-defeating behaviors that previously interfered with the boys' learning and the learning of their classmates.

Ensuring Growth in Best Teaching Practices That Result in High Levels of Learning

Superintendent Freeman recognized the power and impact of collective professional learning and knowledge of all faculty. From the inception of the fledgling Pike Road district, Dr. Freeman established partnerships with several area universities focused on the goal of enhancing the learning experiences for all students in the district. A second goal concentrated on the core belief of continuous learning for all members of Pike Road Schools. Giving evidence to their belief in lifelong learning, faculty and staff committed to improving their professional practice through university–school collaborations that built skills in best instructional strategies, especially in inquiry and investigation of authentic, real-life problems or issues.

Case study leaders understood and valued the knowledge growth of faculty and leaders working together to analyze student data. Faculty from

Tips for Leaders

- Lead faculty in examining instructional/teacher practices on a routine basis throughout the year, and identify areas in need of change. Conduct an instructional audit with a collaborative team.
  - Brainstorm as many instructional practices as possible.
  - Ask faculty to identify the actual practices they use in teaching.
  - Provide evidence to support their use.
  - Collectively identify areas for growth and affirmation.
- Facilitate faculty analyses of student data. Lead faculty in identifying patterns of student performance that indicate a need for intervention, reteaching with new strategies, review of the curriculum, or extensions of the content. Develop specific action steps.
- Lead faculty in identifying and analyzing areas of student learning gaps. Facilitate an examination of past instructional practice that contributed to the gaps, and restructure or expand the instruction for deeper learning. (For lesson study tools, see http://www.tc. columbia.edu/lessonstudy/tools.html.)

these schools and districts applied their learning instantaneously as they examined students' performances and began the process of looking for root causes of gaps in the learning. Data analysis and the *follow-up* to that analysis functioned as a professional learning opportunity that expanded the collective knowledge of team members.

As faculty teams conduct in-depth analyses of gaps in student learning and understanding, patterns emerge from past and present instructional experiences to drive future instruction and close the gaps.

Knowledge learning occurred as faculty analyzed specific omissions in students' learning. Faculty teams identified students' specific instructional gaps, and, without attributing blame or making judgments, they examined the past instructional history of the students. Teams then investigated and identified alternate best practices that supported students in closing their learning gaps. *Once faculty identified specific practices to address the missed learning, teams devoted their common collaborative times to developing their own skills and designing new lessons that addressed the gaps and enhanced the learning process for the students.* The faculty collaboration and professional knowledge building resulted in growth in teaching practices, while students gained a deeper understanding of the concepts.

Leading the Development of Guidelines and Procedures for Learning

Leaders of effective organizations facilitate others in identifying parameters for accomplishing goals and effecting change. Ensuring the alignment of the organization's focus or direction with daily work practices highlights inconsistencies and redirects the actions of the organization. These leaders actively support faculty and staff in creating processes and practices that guide the work of designing profound learning experiences and environments for students. They also address the variety of student needs, identify skills and knowledge for learning, support staff collaboration, and ensure the development of experiential, hands-on learning opportunities.

Leading the Design of Standards-Based Learning that Addresses the Variety of Student Needs

Superintendent Freeman understood that just as students do not always come to school with the requisite knowledge, skills, or abilities for success in school, adults, too, may need to develop the skills or understanding needed to collaborate with their peers in the work place. Pike Road faculty worked together to design environments that inspired students and addressed the variety of student needs. Faculty ensured that their practices provided students with the requisite skills and prior knowledge necessary to access inquiry-focused learning.

Dr. Freeman and the faculty understood the implications resulting from the newness of Pike Road Schools, that all students, faculty, and staff were new to the district and arrived from a wide variety of learning environments and with a range of abilities. Just as faculty developed their instructional practices, they led students in developing practices of learning, such as working in teams, solving problems without easy answers, and understanding that failure is sometimes a part of the path to learning. Faculty ensured that students knew the learning standards and expectations and provided each student with a road map to meet those expectations. Ultimately, Freeman and the Pike Road faculty modeled the excitement of learning new information and caused students to *want to learn* rather than learn only enough to pass the grade level or course.

Tips for Leaders

- Provide professional learning for faculty to deepen their skills of self-reflection about the quality of their work and the variety of student needs.
- Support faculty in developing students' skills of reflecting on their work.
- Effective leaders ensure the use of student practices of learning:
  - Work in teams (collaborate with peers and adults).
  - Stay "in tune" and "on task" with your team.
  - Stay the course (keep trying, even when difficult).
  - Use your imagination (take a risk, follow new ideas).
  - Take suggestions seriously.
  - Listen earnestly to others' thoughts, and question them about their reasoning.
  - Investigate opposing thoughts or ideas.
  - Practice.
  - Draw from past knowledge and experiences.
  - Think about your own thinking. (Why does my solution or creation work? How can I find the answer?)

Chugach School District (CSD) developed a standards-based system of learning and assessment. To move to the next level, students were required to master the previous level at 80% proficiency in every subject. Students helped direct their own learning and assessed the completion of their own goals. In addition, when they mastered the last level, they graduated, regardless of their age—because they met CSD's goals for them and their own goals for themselves.

Effective leaders convene small groups of faculty and community to analyze within and across grade levels the content students must know. They support faculty working in partnership across grade levels and disciplines to encourage all students' natural curiosities for *why* and *how* things work and to find solutions to their questions.

Ensuring the Development of Active, Experiential Learning Opportunities for Students

Tips for Leaders

- Provide professional learning for teachers to deepen their skills in creating inquiry-based lessons (or another active, experiential emphasis).
- Lead discussions that encourage teachers to try new things and step out of their comfort zones when creating lessons.
- Form a partnership with a university to work together to develop active, experiential lessons.

The cliché that *where we spend our money speaks volumes about what we value* is relevant for schools and districts as well as individuals. A sometimes-overlooked facet of developing instructional practices is money expenditure. Disbursements of funds incur a rigorous litmus test and analysis by case study leaders to ensure that all expenditures support student learning and reflect the mission and direction of the organization. Mrs. Tomlinson supported George Hall's faculty by providing students with hands-on activities and authentic problems to solve. With the help of Science, Technology, Engineering, and Mathematics professionals, students built simple machines, developed working Maglev trains, designed turbines and sails to create wind power, and created knee braces. Since many of the students had not traveled beyond their neighborhood, the faculty carefully designed regular field trips that correlated with and deepened the curriculum. Upon returning to the school, students used digital photography to describe the field trip, develop photo stories, and publish them on the Internet. Mrs. Tomlinson ensured that each classroom possessed the necessary tools for experiential learning and investigation, such as computers, interactive white boards, document cameras, and handheld devices.

Students and faculty in Pike Road Schools benefited from the physical location of the district. Situated in a once rural community, Pike Road evolved into a bedroom community of several larger nearby cities and towns. Wetlands, ponds, farming, universities, business, theater, and industry provided possibilities for student exploration and experiential learning. Creation of a completely new public school district afforded the superintendent, faculty, staff, families, and students a once-in-a-lifetime opportunity to invent a more creative and collaborative teaching and learning framework. The Pike Road educational community committed to maintaining their focus on learning as much outside the classroom as inside the classroom. Utilizing the natural resources available to them and enhancing those resources through grant writing, faculty created interconnected learning opportunities through community and business involvement. Students experienced learning in real-time, real-life project-based interactions.

Facilitating an Identification of the Essential Skills and Knowledge Students Must Learn

Tips for Leaders

- Examine the curriculum to ensure not only the inclusion of essential skills but also the ability to expand the learning through inquiry.
- Explore resources in search of experiences that bring learning to life.
- Ask stakeholders and students to identify the essential skills and knowledge students must know.

Case study leaders recognized the importance of involving faculty in continuous evaluation of the quality of instruction and the relevance of the content within their schools. The superintendents and principals demonstrated to faculty the significance of remaining vigilant in providing high-level instruction of important content for the students. They led the restructure of classroom dynamics to promote a collaborative, experience-based environment for learning. The process included assessing the adequacy and alignment of the curriculum across grade levels and content.

Dr. Freeman shared with faculty the forecasts and predictions for the future work world. Analyzing current trends and data concerning employment and the types of employment available in the future caused faculty to rethink their instructional practices and the skills students must know to succeed now and in the future. With their feet planted firmly in today, but with their eyes on the future for their students, Pike Road faculty developed a clear focus on the learning environments created for students.

Creating Opportunities for Faculty to Collaborate on Lessons, Units, and Assessments

Leaders of effective schools and districts recognize that quality instruction that increases student learning does not occur by happenstance. These leaders ensure deliberate and intentional steps so that faculty may develop the lessons, units, experiences, assessments, and projects for their students. They periodically convene teams to review the curriculum and ensure that students receive the necessary support to master essential skills and content.

Ms. Koehn demonstrated the value of faculty collaboration through the implementation of several practices:

- She safeguarded common times for faculty collaboration to create lessons and assessments.

- She participated in weekly meetings of the school leadership team, which included the school instructional coaches for reading and math, psychometrist, counselor, assistant principal, and principal.

- She attended monthly meetings with grade level teams to discuss individual student progress and develop or refine learning plans.

- She protected collaborative time for faculty to analyze their lessons prior to and following implementation and to reflect on the students' learning.

- She received commitments from all faculty and staff and newly hired faculty to participate in summer professional learning.

Tips for Leaders

Schedule regular collaboration time for faculty to meet during the school day. Schools have found a number of effective ways to do this:

- Schedule the same lunch period for faculty groups with a preparation period immediately after.

- Provide students with service learning time, and allow faculty to collaborate during that time.

- Move to a year-round calendar, with inter-sessions that allow faculty collaboration.

- Dismiss classes early a specific number of days.

- Schedule art, music, physical education, etc. during the same time, and provide faculty collaboration sessions during that time.

- Redeploy staff or use grants to hire additional faculty.

Critical Practice 4

Give Life to Data

Leaders in high-performing organizations oversee the analysis of key data and make sure that data and current research are used to improve student learning. They communicate key data to stakeholders, using a variety of methods to ensure understanding. Data, to these leaders, are not static, tedious facts to be endured, but comprise dynamic, interesting, and *living pieces of information* that create wisdom and benefit everyone.

> It is essential that leaders work to establish a culture where results are carefully assessed and actions are taken based on these assessments.
>
> (Schlechty, 2005, p. 11)

Ensuring That Key Data Are Analyzed in a Deliberate Manner

Effective data analysis uncovers connections, trends, and patterns useful in making successful decisions. Moreover, relevant data, collected and analyzed in an organized manner, establish a sense of confidence in the results.

As outstanding leaders work toward world-class achievement, data that focus on results guide their decisions. Their improvement efforts are most successful when the decision-making process is highly data driven. In these schools and districts, leaders make sure the appropriate data are available, maintain a schedule that provides time for collaborative data analysis, review data analysis and use on a regular basis, and ensure the use of effective data analysis tools.

Data analysis is not the job of just one person. The leadership team, faculty, and staff work together to select, gather, analyze, manage, and improve school data and knowledge resources.

Ensuring the Availability of Data and Information

It is the leader's responsibility to ensure the availability of useful data.

Gathering data and making it available should be a deliberate process, regularly implemented, and planned to make sure the data are useful for decision-making. Useful data will guide leaders, faculty, staff, students, and parents in ensuring appropriate student learning.

According to Victoria Bernhardt (2004), four types of collected data indicate school and district success: student learning data, perception data, demographic data, and school process data. Student learning data may include annual state assessments, formative standardized assessments taken throughout the academic year, ongoing faculty-made assessments, periodic student self-assessment, and other types of learning evaluations. Perception data usually include satisfaction and/or awareness surveys of parents, students, school and district personnel, and other stakeholders. Demographic data often include information about students and their parents, enrollment rates in programs, student behavioral and social problems, parent involvement data, and mobility patterns. Process data encompass many areas, such as collaboration, leadership, program implementation, building cleanliness, and financial procedures. There are other models of data collection and use, but these four main types are specific yet broad enough to ensure that useful data and information are included.

Tips for Leaders

- Student achievement data are clearly the most important to collect and analyze, but there are also other data types that are informative and useful when planning for student success, some of which are:
  - demographic information;
  - mobility patterns of grades and schools;
  - rates of enrollments in various programs;
  - parent involvement;
  - behavior and social problems of students; and
  - perception data of all stakeholders.
- Collect data over a multi-year period so trends will be apparent; use data from the same sources over time when possible; and make sure multiple measures are available.

At Hastings Middle School in Hastings, Nebraska, Principal *David Essink* ensured the availability of data for faculty, who used data from EXPLORE tests, the Cognitive Aptitude Test, and the Measures of Academic Progress. Faculty used formative assessment data to make changes in instruction, and students set goals for themselves and monitored their own results. Pre-tests and post-tests provided baseline information and demonstrated growth.

At Alice Ott Middle School, Principal Johnston ensured that student and school data were available for continuous use. He and faculty so closely monitored student data that they knew when any student was ready to move to the next level. Rather than waiting until the end of each semester, Mr. Johnston moved students to a higher level class as soon as they were ready.

Leaders in the Chugach School District (CSD) ensured the availability of data for formative and summative purposes. They used student performance data, student work, graduation rates, college entrance rates, stakeholder surveys, the Alaska State Report Card, and Alaska Benchmark and High School Qualifying Examination results. They benchmarked key performance indicators and disseminated data summaries to the school board and to stakeholder groups. CSD's Aligned Information Management System (AIMS) ensured that leaders, faculty, students, and parents were able to monitor student progress in meeting standards in real time and included dashboard indicators of student-learning targets. Reports were available at the student, group, and district level.

Providing Regular Opportunities to Collaboratively Analyze Key Data

Tips for Leaders

- Identify a data team with members from the school or district and the wider community to lead the data collection and analysis.
- Make sure that data are available for the team in an easy-to-access format.
- Develop, with the team, a plan that identifies protocols for data collection and analysis, with target dates and persons responsible.
- Spend some time clarifying problems. It is often helpful for teams to identify the problems that need to be resolved, and then develop a hypothesis, evidence, and an action plan for each problem.

Leaders who structure regular times for teams to assess student work provide the foundation for a collaborative culture where everyone is responsible for student learning. Mrs. Tomlinson consistently led George Hall faculty in analyzing student data and posted the data in prominent locations throughout the school. She analyzed student data *every day*; faculty frequently assessed students; and students monitored their own data. The George Hall team room provided an always-available place for faculty and leaders to collaborate in analyzing data.

At Scott Morgan Johnson Middle School in McKinney, Texas, Principal *Mitchell Curry* provided time for subject-area faculty to work together from three to five times each week to evaluate data, discuss strategies, and design common formative assessments. Other teams of faculty collaborated in a number of areas, including tracking student progress, designing interventions, and setting up flexible student groupings.

In 2013, Scott Johnson was the highest-achieving school in the district, even though it was the school with the largest number of high-need students, and was named a 2013 MetLife–NASSP Breakthrough School for its academic success (NASSP, 2012).

Ensuring the Use of Effective Tools to Analyze Key Data Collaboratively

Data provide knowledge of the strengths and weaknesses of individual students and of the school and district, set the foundation for rewarding success and acknowledging areas for improvement, and ensure the solution of the basic causes of problems rather than simply obscuring symptoms.

Tips for Leaders

- Provide professional learning opportunities for teachers covering the effective use of data tools.
- Talk often about specific data analysis tools used in the school or district.
- Create a chart showing which tools are used most effectively to analyze various kinds of data.

Figure 11.1 The PDSA Cycle

Leadership teams often use a defined and structured improvement process to increase student learning and improve programs and processes.

Many organizations use a Plan–Do–Study–Act (PDSA), sometimes called the Plan–Do–Check–Act (PDCA), cycle for continuous improvement to analyze key data and make improvements. The PDSA cycle is a simple, but highly effective, four-stage model for planning, analysis, and action.

Plan
Identify the need for change, and plan for implementation.
Do
Carry out a pilot study to assess the effectiveness of the change.
Study
Analyze the results and identify what worked and what did not work.
Act
Take action based on what you learned in the previous step. If the change was not effective, revise the plan. If the change was effective, use it to make broader systemic changes. Return to the first step to design new changes, initiating the cycle again.

Charts like the PDSA Action Plan below often assist leaders in guiding the process and ensuring the successful implementation of each stage.

PDSA Action Plan			
	What	Who	When
Plan			
Do			
Study			
Act			

When school or district teams collect and analyze data before developing solutions, the outcome has a greater chance of success. Faculty at George Hall Elementary School used the Plan–Do–Check–Act improvement cycle to review data and make improvements during their twice-weekly meetings.

To focus on continuous improvement, CSD developed the PIER (Plan, Implement, Evaluate, and Refine) process. Faculty, staff, leaders, students, and stakeholders used PIER Plans to assess meeting their goals and to identify areas for improvement. Every level used PIER Plans. Students' PIER Plans were called individual learning plans and helped them manage their own learning. PIER was also part of the CSD's strategic planning process.

Some of the other tools often used to analyze key data are check sheets, histograms, cause and effect diagrams, flowcharts, run charts, affinity diagrams, Pareto charts, tree diagrams, force field analysis, how-how diagrams, and nominal group technique. Appendix A includes links to descriptions of each of these tools.

Reviewing Data Analysis and Use on a Regular Basis

Leaders of high-performing organizations regularly, often continuously, monitor the use and analysis of data. It is critical, of course, for leaders to review the data in order to know student learning progress and the effectiveness of various processes. However, to keep a focus on direction, leaders should also review the data analysis and use by teams and others.

Tips for Leaders

- Create systematic, straightforward, easy-to-use processes for gathering and displaying data that everyone understands.
- Facilitate regular data meetings held often throughout the year.
- Ensure that leadership team data meetings are held regularly and often.

CSD leaders reviewed AIMS dashboard indicators each month in order to make sure that learning was occurring at the appropriate levels.

Faculty and students reviewed student progress between and within levels. CSD information was also used to benchmark, track goals, identify gaps, and celebrate successes.

At Alice Ott Middle School, Principal Johnston reviewed student achievement and behavior through color-coded spreadsheets he created. In addition to using the data to move students to different classes as soon as they were ready, leaders tracked student discipline issues and conducted early interventions before behaviors became continuing problems.

George Hall Elementary School Principal Terri Tomlinson analyzed student data every day, and faculty assessed students frequently. "We have had steady gains every year, but to do that, we had to be data driven, and we had to review the data regularly and often," Tomlinson explained.

Using Data and Current Research to Improve Student Learning

12

According to EMC/International Data Corporation's 2014 Digital Universe Study, the amount of data available for use is doubling every two years and, by 2020, will reach 44 trillion gigabytes. There is no doubt that, at the simplest level, this is enough data. The dilemma we face is how much of it is appropriate for use and how much of it will make a difference. In 2013, only 22% of the world's data was useful for decision-making purposes. The predicted percentage growth in useful data by 2020 is approximately 35% (Digital Universe, 2014). Clearly, it is critical to determine which data are high value in that they will support student learning, best teaching practices, and school improvement.

In high-performing schools and districts, the leader makes sure the data that are used are relevant to improved student learning and school improvement. Leaders regularly connect teaching practices and student data, ensure data-based development of teaching strategies, and focus on recent research and its implications for teaching.

Facilitating Faculty Conversations about Connections between Teaching Practices and Student Data

Education leaders often encourage faculty to use data to identify necessary changes in teaching practices. However, in addition to encouragement, faculty need opportunities to exchange ideas with colleagues and to enrich their experience through in-depth conversations about these connections. Case study leaders made sure faculty had time and support to talk about data and the resulting changes to their teaching practices. For example, they created schedules where faculty met regularly each week in data meetings to review the data, discuss implications, plan for changes in practice, and examine resulting implementation.

Faculty discussions about data analysis were an integral and routine part of the work of Winterboro High School. Principal Bates led the Winterboro faculty in analyzing data by facilitating Teacher Academy each Friday during faculty preparation periods. Monthly standards-based assessments for students provided faculty with important data concerning student progress, and any student failing to score a mastery percentage received additional instruction in a new way in workshop or small group formats. In addition to these locally developed assessments, faculty used regular benchmark Discovery Education assessments and school district mathematics benchmarks to identify needs for targeted assistance. They disaggregated and analyzed data, discussed the results, and used the data to plan instruction.

Tips for Leaders

- Create opportunities for faculty to visit other schools or districts that are successfully using data and research to improve student learning. Charge a faculty team with identifying places to visit.
- Create opportunities for faculty to visit each other and observe successful teaching practices that changed based on data.

Whenever faculty observed a student struggling in understanding of content or performance on assessments, Mr. Bates asked the questions: "How do we help these students? What does this mean to us as a staff? What does this indicate to us?" Then he supported the faculty in developing a plan for the student.

Ensuring the Development of Teaching Strategies in Response to the Data

Insightful leaders encourage a systematic and collaborative process of data interpretation among colleagues to gain insight into student learning.

Tips for Leaders

- Ask faculty regularly, "What is the latest change in your practice you made based on data?"
- Allocate part of each faculty meeting to a discussion of this issue.
- Identify a faculty team that will collect descriptions of changes in practice based on data and/or research; charge the team with recognizing and celebrating these changes.

Teams look for patterns of high performance and patterns of deficiencies in learning across individual student data, grade level data, school data, and district data. As faculty teams discuss student performance and strategize about next steps, they formulate instructional interventions and practices focused on improving student learning. They frequently revisit the time allocated to learning in students' areas of greatest need. Leaders guide faculty in sharing best practices for the most difficult to teach concepts and using those practices to create strategies that specifically address students' identified learning gaps. Faculty obtain valuable data to help assess the effectiveness of the learning process by reviewing the

- instructional format;
- structure of the learning environment;
- time frame devoted to identified areas of concern;
- order of introduction for certain concepts; and
- effectiveness of instructional practices.

Faculty at Hewitt-Trussville Middle School studied their own student data and those of the school as a whole. They analyzed the specific concepts that reflected poor student performance and assessed the instructional time devoted to those concepts. The findings provided teams with insight into relationships between time allocated to learning new concepts and student understanding. Faculty teams evaluated teaching strategies and last year's lesson plans to determine root causes of student performance, and then designed new lessons that addressed specific weaknesses.

Following the data analysis, faculty also designed lessons that targeted specific areas identified in the analysis as poor performance.

Dr. Faust facilitated a faculty analysis of each week's list of students who had a grade D or F (D/F list). Every member on each team received the team's entire D/F list and assumed ownership for the success of all students on their team. They talked through each individual student's situation with counselors and administrators to discuss accommodations or strategies to help students achieve success.

At Garner Magnet High School, the mission of the instructional support team (IST) was to ensure academic success for all students through supporting best practices throughout the school. The IST also gathered data and reviewed instructional practices to identify professional development needs. The regular meetings of Garner faculty, as they reviewed data, discussed issues, and solved problems together, consistently delivered innovative ideas for teaching and learning and further use of data.

Focusing on Recent Research in the Field and Implications for Instruction

Educators need access to recent research and the opportunity to discuss and practice it on a regular and ongoing basis. Leaders of high-performing schools and districts arrange schedules to provide this access and opportunity. They also organize meetings so that conversations about research and its implications for instruction are the central focus of the meetings rather than logistical issues that would benefit from another conversation or form of communication.

Tips for Leaders

- Use email rather than faculty meetings to cover logistical issues.
- Charge a faculty team with reviewing research, either generally or in specific areas, and suggesting research-based practices to the entire faculty.

Kevin Grawer transformed the way Maplewood Richmond Heights faculty meetings were held. The school rarely had an all-school faculty meeting; usually smaller, focused committees discussed research and best practices, solved problems, made decisions, and then shared their findings and recommendations. "We value people's time, and are committed to getting something done, so when we have meetings, there will be action results," Mr. Grawer said.

At Alice Ott Middle School, faculty and leaders consulted current research as they developed programs targeting improved student learning. For example, the leadership team used data to identify an achievement gap among students and developed a new system *to engage parents and all faculty members* in reducing the achievement gap. To create a successful system, the team visited schools that were performing well in this area and researched numerous programs. The literacy team regularly reviewed current research and suggested research-based practices for faculty to try. Faculty then led school-wide literacy meetings and shared evidence of implementation and results with colleagues. They used these meetings to discuss ideas and talk about what worked and possible strategies for doing things differently.

Ensuring that Data Used Impact Student Learning

Tips for Leaders

- Provide professional development for faculty on which types of data to use for different purposes. This will likely need presentation time over the course of an academic year.

- Analyze data that show student success or lack of success in various areas in addition to assessment results. Lead faculty in identifying these additional data to analyze.

- When anyone requests a resource, the development of a new program, or any other change, ask them to present the data that show how it will improve student learning.

- Connect with educators at other schools and school districts to share data and strategies.

The most critical use of data is to increase student learning. Administrators and faculty in high-performing schools and districts use data to understand students' academic needs and respond to them through targeted instruction and support. Ultimately, data in these organizations inform instruction and help create changes in teaching practices.

Scott Morgan Johnson Middle School leaders, faculty, and staff believed that student failure was not an option. Consequently, students were required to demonstrate mastery, often choosing from a menu of assessment opportunities. Faculty and students used comprehensive performance data to design individual student academic goals and action plans. Students who did not demonstrate mastery were provided with additional instruction.

The Chugach School District's (CSD) assessment system included content and process skills in ten content areas. Before moving to the next level, students demonstrated proficiency (80% mastery) on an assessment, which included the students' reflection on their learning, a skills assessment of specific content, and a performance assessment, often co-designed with the students. CSD's common grading system incorporated Emerging, Developing, Proficient, and Advanced levels. AIMS tracked this entire process. CSD Superintendent Bob Crumley said:

> State assessments are snapshots. We have performance-based assessments and use them to determine exactly where students are and what their progress has been. Student performance levels are often a minimum for graduation. Our standards go above and beyond that and prepare students for success after graduation.

Three of the teams at Garner Magnet High School saw the need to evaluate data concerning student failures. The leadership team, the instructional support team, and the school improvement team each reviewed failure data. Each team, individually, determined that there were a higher number of failures among freshmen. Team members talked with professional learning teams and discovered that students were failing most often because they were not turning in their work. In addition, the data showed, as did current research, that freshmen students failing more than one course dropped out of school at a higher rate than students without multiple failures. All teams decided to make this issue an action area for improvement, thus ensuring that the data they used impacted student learning.

13 | Communicating Key Data to All Stakeholders

In high-performing schools and districts, leaders make sure all relevant data are available, visible, and clear to stakeholders. Leaders establish processes to deploy the data, help stakeholders understand it, and communicate regularly with stakeholders about the data.

Data conveyed to stakeholders should communicate important and relevant information. Consequently, effective leaders utilize key data in communication with stakeholders, rather than every data point possible. Stakeholders can help determine which data are key and which are non-essential.

Ensuring Transparency and Clarity of the Data

Tips for Leaders

- Provide regular data in a format that staff can use to make decisions about student learning and success. Ask staff what format would be most helpful.
- Use graphics to ensure clarity of data.
- Make sure that resources related to data and measures are in one place on the website. Ensure easy navigability of the website.

Data shared with stakeholders represent a powerful change agent for good. Leaders of high-performing schools and districts use transparent and visible data to analyze the levels of student learning and the quality of programs and processes. Leaders present these data in an easy-to-understand format.

At Trenton High School in Trenton, Missouri, faculty called Principal *Dan Wiebers* "Data Dan." Wiebers provided faculty with quarterly statistical data reports, including data organized in such a way that they could be used to modify instruction. He used data to create positive change in the school as well as to celebrate successes and identify areas of concern. Faculty used the data he provided to ascertain which students needed help, set target goals for students, identify problems, and implement solutions. "My best teachers had a grasp of their classroom data and made educated decisions using that data," Wiebers said. "Students were allowed to track their own data, and the classroom was a positive learning environment for all of the students." The results were exceptional. Student achievement and graduation rate increased significantly. The school received the state of Missouri's Distinction in Performance recognition and was named a 2012 MetLife–NASSP Breakthrough School for its academic success.

Establishing Processes to Deploy Key Data to Stakeholders

Data deployment in education is sometimes intermittent and based on state agency or accreditation requirements. Effective leaders establish regular processes for the deployment of key data to stakeholders and involve stakeholders in identifying the data to share.

Effective leaders also ensure data are disseminated to stakeholders in a variety of ways. Not all recipients use social media, but social media is all that some people use, so multiple methods of deployment will help important information reach everyone. A variety of deployment methods will also make sure that no stakeholders are left out and that *each stakeholder group receives the data they want*. This is a step often neglected by educational organizations. A spreadsheet like the one below will help leaders deploy data in an organized and useful manner.

Stakeholder Group	Data Type	Target Deployment Dates	Person Responsible

Tips for Leaders

Schools and districts can deploy data and information to stakeholders in a variety of ways:

- Develop clear and informative websites.
- Use multiple social media, such as Twitter, Facebook, LinkedIn, YouTube, and blogs.
- Implement parent/stakeholder data nights, where teachers *and students* explain data.
- Identify specific stakeholders as ambassadors who can share and explain data.
- Hold meetings to clarify specialized data to specific groups.
- Convene focus groups for the purpose of gathering and sharing data.
- Send regular emails and newsletters to stakeholders.
- Give interviews and quotes to print and broadcast media.

The Chugach School District (CSD) sent out a general newsletter every other month, regular program newsletters designed to update stakeholders, and annual strategic newsletters that described strategic plan goals and progress. An annual report card to the public and letters to each community kept stakeholders informed about student, school, and district progress. Parents and students, the primary stakeholders, had access to CSD's AIMS data so they could monitor student progress in real time online.

The Pewaukee School District continuously updated graphs and charts of student progress on its website to keep stakeholders informed and included. School publications, district newsletters, an annual report, school newsletters, websites, the district electronic calendar, Facebook, and Twitter were used to disseminate information to stakeholders. Comments and Likes provided feedback to help PSD personnel understand and respond to stakeholders' interests.

Developing Stakeholder Understanding of Key Data

Sending data to stakeholders is not helpful, valuable, or practical unless they understand the data and their uses. *Leaders must ensure stakeholder understanding.* Leaders of high-performing organizations have created various ways to make sure stakeholders understand the data and information they receive.

Tips for Leaders

- Use multiple methods to help stakeholders understand the data they will receive *prior to* its dissemination.

- Include stakeholders on committees that determine the needed data and design the data deployment methods.

- Define measures and data points in all documents and online clearly and *consistently*. Define terms that may be unknown to some stakeholders.

- Make sure that data are updated in a timely manner in all resources.

CSD's individual learning plans for all students provided continuous and up-to-date information about student progress, and parent conferences ensured parental understanding of the learning plans. In addition, the annual letters to each community clarified in detail the annual report cards sent to stakeholders.

At Winterboro High School, Principal Bates provided key data to stakeholders and held meetings to ensure their understanding. George Hall Elementary School leaders visited every student's home to ensure understanding. Wayne Richardson, principal of Deer Valley Elementary School, sent frequent explanatory emails to students' parents ensuring understanding of school information and actions.

Communicating with Stakeholders about Data

Communicating with stakeholders about data does not mean simply telling them what the data show. Communicating with stakeholders about data involves sharing the data and then using stakeholder input and feedback as a beginning point for conversations about needed improvements. In addition, many stakeholders have areas of expertise that would be helpful in analyzing data, planning for improvement, and conveying information to other stakeholders. They could, for example, serve on data teams, help write grants and proposals, speak to the media, review research, and evaluate data.

Tips for Leaders

Lead a data roundtable to bring a large group of stakeholders together. Use the roundtable to establish credibility, find common ground, share important information, and make sure stakeholders are on the same page regarding goals and data communication.

Stakeholder communication about data generally produces stakeholder ownership in problems that regularly arise in schools and districts. The Chugach community's sense of ownership of their schools resulted originally from their review of the data and their communication about the data with school personnel and other stakeholders.

Garner Magnet High School identified cross-functional teams for each improvement plan key process. The teams gathered and analyzed data, shared results, and worked together toward the overarching goal of every Garner student graduating. Principal Cook believed that when stakeholders' ideas are validated and used, they remain supportive and involved in the improvement process (National Association of Secondary School Principals, 2014b).

Critical Practice 5
Lead Learning

Effective leaders continuously learn and create an environment that encourages the same in others. Leaders of high-performing schools and districts have the skills and knowledge to keep well informed and up to date on current trends and to design experiences for others to deepen their learning. They create ongoing daily learning experiences, challenge the status quo, and support innovation.

Establishing an Environment of Daily Learning for All

Today's educators must adapt to meet demands that are continuously changing and expanding, leading a shift from teaching to learning. The questions posed by these changes often have no obvious answers (Heifetz and Laurie, 1997), requiring administrators, faculty, and staff to continuously expand their own abilities through systematic processes for sharing knowledge. Effective leaders model and reward collaboration, reflection, and knowledge sharing.

Modeling Collaboration, Reflection, and Knowledge Sharing in Daily Practice

Tips for Leaders

- Establish a process of faculty reflection on current and past practices. Collectively assess the group's progress in the change process.

- Lead faculty teams in reviewing the recently taught lesson of a colleague and providing constructive feedback to enhance the lesson. (Identify a volunteer to share the lesson prior to the team meeting.)

- Protect faculty and staff collaborative time and devote it to sharing knowledge and creating rich learning experiences for students.

- Actively lead faculty in abandoning lessons, practices, or procedures that no longer meet the needs of today's students or advance learning.

Principal Faust recognized the importance of faculty developing together the common knowledge and language of teaching math. Teacher-leaders facilitated monthly PLC sessions to support each mathematics teacher's ability and conceptual understanding of numeracy. In addition, a book study, in conjunction with developing the skill of leading number talks, created a cohesive and collegial learning community that spoke the same "language" and shared the same learning journey. The outcome of the experience for faculty was a common ownership and sense of responsibility for the entire middle school mathematics curriculum.

A common theme or characteristic of effective leadership that models knowledge sharing and self-reflection is the commitment to incorporate knowledge sharing into every aspect of the organization's work. Reflecting on current and past practices, analyzing the effectiveness of a recent lesson, deepening an understanding of inquiry-based learning, and gathering the voices of students about their learning have little meaning unless faculty actually apply the newly developed skills and philosophical shifts. Hewitt-Trussville faculty valued their daily collaborative time devoted to lesson design and redesign and shared insights learned from the collective mind of the group. The real test of the significance of the learning experiences occurred when faculty transferred the knowledge into action and supported their colleagues to do the same.

As difficult as it was for some, Hewitt-Trussville faculty put aside personal instructional preferences and the "tried and true" lessons of many years. They embraced the open door to meaningful dialogue about students' learning in depth rather than students' previous superficial learning. Collegial conversations encouraged faculty to voice their concerns— or their enthusiasm—about letting go of former lesson plans (some on paper yellowed from years of use) to develop new formats for learning that reflected the world around them. To ensure worthy use of the designated time for faculty collaboration, Hewitt-Trussville followed a weekly schedule focused on sharing and reflection that developed teaching practices.

Monday: Lesson Plan Protocol—Following a protocol, faculty collectively reviewed and discussed the week's lesson plans, providing suggestions and feedback for colleagues.

Tuesday: Grade Analysis—Faculty asked themselves the question: "When students are not succeeding, what will I build into the work that will support their learning and provide for success?"

Wednesday: Collaborative Lesson Plan—Faculty teams created lessons or units of study and then expanded their thinking and developed the proposed lessons by implementing coaching circles to ask "what if" questions about the lessons.

Thursday: Protocols—Faculty followed protocols to examine samples of student work and analyze the quality of the assignments as well as student performance.

Leading a Shift from a Focus on Teaching to a Focus on Learning

Leaders of high-performing schools and districts know that time for reflection is a necessary component for understanding new learning. Leaders also understand the imperative of creating an atmosphere that supports collaboration among faculty and staff, a setting where learning is an essential part of each day's work. Mindful leaders recognize the importance of reflecting on current and past practices, building trusting relationships among faculty and staff, and maintaining a state of *perpetual renewal* to achieve school success (Kearney et al., 2013).

Tips for Leaders

- Facilitate conversations with faculty to deepen the understanding of the shift in focus from teaching to learning. Select a strategy from Appendix A to guide the discussion.

- Lead faculty teams in an assessment of the culture of the school or district. Identify key reinforcers to maintain the culture of learning.

- Facilitate conversations to validate newly acquired practices. Provide support and direction for those reluctant to change. Remind them that the newly learned practices support the direction of the school or district.

- Provide journal articles about student engagement prior to a discussion. Ask staff to share a previous learning experience. Identify the common points of the various experiences. Compare them to an engaging learning experience described in the journal article.

Historically, teaching, learning, and growth in student understanding and achievement placed the teacher "front and center" as the primary focus of classroom practices. Leaders who are facilitating a shift in focus from faculty to students and their learning recognize that some faculty may experience a sense of loss for the practices that worked for them in the past. Faculty may also feel confused about which new practices will work. Many candid, but respectful, discussions in protected settings encourage faculty to communicate their concerns and reflect on these philosophical and practical changes. Effective leaders understand that as faculty experience the freedom and safety of sharing their anxieties about this change of focus with their peers, they grow in their understanding of the *perpetual renewal* described by Kearney et al. (2013).

An important component for several of the case study schools was the dedication of collaborative team time to the practice of following protocols to guide discussions. The discussions addressed practices such as lesson plans, grade analysis, and lesson design, asking *what if* or *have you thought about* questions, and tackled investigations of the impact of instruction on student learning. Observant principals and superintendents realized the strength of supporting faculty as they looked at their own practices and grappled with new insights about their personal instructional needs as well as the needs of students. Protected daily time for faculty dialogue provided the platform for growth in faculty learning, which transferred to a focus on student learning rather than on the teaching act itself.

Principal Essink recognized the critical importance and power of Hastings Middle School faculty working in collaborative teams to change the direction of the school and improve student performance. Faculty teams supported one another in building their knowledge base of the state standards while creating curriculum guides to support their work. Faculty realized that if they did not fully comprehend the content of the high-stakes testing, it would be difficult to deepen student understanding. Faculty held themselves to a high standard and committed to build their knowledge of the assessments as well as to gain a solid awareness of the expectations of the next grade level. Principal Essink created a school schedule that supported faculty collaborative teamwork. Teams met in common planning times to design structures and processes that supported the learning of students. Essink also found other times for faculty teams to collaborate in knowledge building and to share their goals and new strategies with him.

Another example of focusing on the learning rather than the teaching at Hastings came in the form of additional contract time for faculty to collaborate with their learning teams. Weekly early school dismissal at 2:30 provided another protected time for faculty to focus on student learning. Asking themselves "how do we know if students have learned the information and what do we do if they don't know it?" drove their work. Faculty teams soon realized their lessons had not engaged the students. Essink encouraged the teams as they studied *student engagement* and shared with the entire faculty new approaches to learning and developing lessons that engaged students. Hastings demonstrated changes in their school culture from a place of teaching to a place of collaboration and learning. Student achievement increased significantly, and Hastings was named a 2014 MetLife–NASSP Breakthrough School for its academic success (NASSP, 2013).

Rewarding Formal and Informal Collaboration and Knowledge Sharing

Tips for Leaders

- Publicly affirm the hard work of the faculty as they explore and implement changes in their practice.
- Develop, with faculty and staff, a system of recognition and rewards for collaboration and knowledge sharing.

The superintendents and principals in these case studies consistently concentrated on sharing knowledge throughout the school and district and within the community of parents and businesses. As faculty investigated appropriate avenues of instruction that helped students learn at higher levels, observant leaders provided opportunities for sharing experiences and new knowledge. Faculty and parent meetings, focus groups, and Board of Education meetings, as well as school memos and personal notes to faculty, afforded leaders opportunities to highlight faculty efforts and encouraged them to share their successes and growth in their practice. Faculty-led conversations described to parents and colleagues the experiences of exploring changes in practice that resulted in increased student learning. The conversations rewarded and affirmed faculty for their work and informed the faculty and parents of their commitment to growing as professionals. As principals asked faculty to share at least one new concept or strategy learned at a professional conference, the principal demonstrated the importance of lifelong learning while faculty gained new knowledge, and the conversations validated their experiences.

Maintaining Systematic Processes for Sharing Knowledge

In the schools and districts mentioned in these case studies, the direction of the organizations shifted away from a faculty and staff focus to a student-focused powerful organization. Faculty comments reflected the transformations that occurred over time at each school.

A fourth-grade teacher at George Hall described changes in the school's processes over time:

> When I walked into my classroom as a first-year teacher, it was totally unlike what I expected: it was fully stocked with math manipulatives, reading resources, and any supplies imagined. A mentor teacher was in my room for the first three weeks of school. She provided guidance about discipline, school culture, and all the necessary paperwork. Besides giving me confidence, she worked with me throughout the year to ensure my success.

In addition, a second-grade teacher described the transformation:

> I remember that first year at George Hall, how we had to go out into the homes and make sure that the students came to school. Attendance is very important. We would call and tell the parents that we needed the student here at school, please bring them. Sometimes the parents or students would say they didn't have a clean uniform, but we took care of that matter by supplying them with one. We just could not let them stay at home when their education was on the line. We worked hard those first few years, and it showed in the success of the students. They became

learners and they wanted to learn. Now, they value education as much as we do as teachers. They have grasped the concept that in order to be successful in life, education is the key. Nine years later, we still share our knowledge with each other, and we still hold those same values as we did in the beginning. We still work hard and we believe in educating the whole child and community. No matter how many awards and accolades we receive, there is nothing greater than the success of a child.

Tips for Leaders

Facilitate teams in completing the school or district inventory found in Appendix C.

- Discuss similarities and differences in perceptions.
- Identify areas of greatest disparity and discuss the significance of the differences.

A seventh grade teacher described how the teachers changed Hewitt-Trussville. "We work very hard, constantly sharing ideas, and it is no accident that we have evolved to the school we are now." She added that the faculty knows how they were able to make such significant growth. "Dr. Faust leads by example and models what she believes. She never asks anything of us that she has not already done. She is a wonderful leader."

Principal Bates consistently and regularly maintained knowledge sharing processes. The superintendent stated that the work at Winterboro "exceeds the norms of traditional teaching and learning through innovative instructional methods to better prepare students for life after graduation." A faculty member added that "the one thing that stands out about our instruction . . . is the level of student engagement." A student echoed the superintendent and faculty comments when he stated that "twenty-first century skills involve more than just projects. We are building self-worth, community mindedness, and taking responsibility for our own actions through projects."

Challenging the Status Quo and Working with Others to Achieve Change Goals

Change that happens quickly encourages leaders to place high value on creating capacity, on the ability to anticipate, engage in, and benefit from all kinds of situations. Leaders of effective schools and districts are expert at challenging the status quo, using knowledge to innovate, asking the right questions and listening to the answers, and creating a sense of urgency about change. At the same time, they understand that change often causes a sense of loss when people have to give up the familiar, the way they learned to function, or the security of knowing exactly what to do next. Therefore, the creation of a culture of caring, communication, and collaboration found in the Focus on Direction practice (Critical Practice 1) is critical. Without a clear understanding of the direction of the organization and without a commitment to the direction, schools and districts sometimes trip and fall away from their goals as changes ruffle feathers among faculty and staff. Future-oriented, capable leadership keeps faculty and staff focused on change goals, removes barriers, and supports and coaches faculty in moving outside their comfort zone for the sake of student learning. Such leaders encourage conversations about new ideas and *lead the learning*.

Inviting Different Perspectives from Others by Asking the Right Questions and Listening to the Answers

A primary function of leadership is to produce positive change. For today's schools to do more than survive, but to thrive, flexibility and openness to change are imperative. Leaders of high-performing schools and districts know how to ask the right questions—and to listen to the answers. Principal Koehn led the learning and change process at Kennedy Elementary by continually asking the right questions and listening to the responses. Asking how and why questions prompted faculty to think deeply about the questions and provide meaningful replies. Questions and the conversations that followed served as catalysts for reflections concerning the work of learning and the possibilities for real and significant change on behalf of students.

Chugach School District's (CSD) Superintendent Crumley modeled asking the right questions and listened to the community's answers. The changes that occurred after considerable thought and dialogue among colleagues paved the way for CSD to create an entirely new approach to teaching and learning.

Tips for Leaders

- Asking questions provides an opportunity for others to present issues or make suggestions they may not otherwise voice.

- In addition to why, where, when, who, and how, include questions such as:

  - What is your goal for this lesson?

  - What is it about the new direction that you like (or do not like)?

  - What do you see as your role or responsibility in our organization?

Creating a Sense of Urgency about Positive Change and Improvement in Every Area

Forward-thinking leaders grasp the significance of the adage *everything that occurs during the school day (from the time students get on the school bus in the morning until they get off the bus in the afternoon), as well as before and after the school day (at home and at work), is a part of the learning experience and process.* The former superintendent of the Mountain Brook School District in Mountain Brook, Alabama, *Charles Mason,* recognized the importance of all personnel as part of the learning community. He transformed an understanding of the roles of staff, including custodians, school nutrition workers, and grounds keepers. Stakeholders recognized that without a safe school structure, learning floundered. Without a clean school, the health of students suffered. Without nutritious lunches, hunger derailed the learning. With ill-equipped labs and faulty learning tools, the wonder of science remained a mystery. Stakeholders embraced the concept that everyone in and around the school and district influenced the teaching and learning process. Faculty and staff in every area of the Mountain Brook learning community committed themselves to re-visioning their roles and responsibilities as essential parts of a strong and supportive learning environment. Finally, support staff were included in the annual awards ceremony.

Tips for Leaders

- Create a sense of urgency for positive change by reminding stakeholders that the experiences of students today set the path for the remainder of their lives.

- Ensure that all faculty and staff understand their roles in creating change. Facilitate a conversation that emphasizes the importance of each person in supporting the strong learning community.

- Develop a description of the status of student learning and the probable demands facing students in the future. Give examples that connect emotionally with stakeholders.

Informed leaders understand that real change occurs only through open and honest dialogue among the stakeholders (Kotter and Cohen, 2002). The importance of identifying the "problem" and building an understanding of the need for change requires speaking to others' emotions. By speaking truthfully about the status of student learning and the reduced probability of students' future successes without changes, leaders can connect with other stakeholders and build a culture of trust. Stakeholders, sensing the urgency for action, connect with the need for change and the desire to make a difference.

Empowering Others to Remove Barriers to Change

Can schools and districts overcome barriers to implementing plans for improvement? What are the barriers to significant change in organizations? Many volumes of educational journals recount the importance of developing a vision and mission, creating a new culture of learning, communicating plans to all stakeholders, and numerous other imperatives. Little space, however, is devoted to outlining specifics for removing barriers to the implementation of change initiatives or plans for improvement. Effective school and district leaders know that identification of the "stumbling blocks" to improved learning and the creation of plans for making needed changes are the first and easiest steps toward increased learning. The difficult task is the implementation of plans. The act of implementing plans for improved learning often requires seismic shifts in the multifaceted structure and beliefs of a school or district.

Tips for Leaders

- Ensure a climate of trust and collegiality that encourages and applauds innovative thinking.
- Recognize faculty and staff and stakeholders who remove barriers to change.

The same stakeholders, once on board with the plans, may then resist and jeopardize the implementation of changes. An effective leader recognizes the perceived threats inherent in any change in direction and works to allay fears through honest discourse. Fears present themselves in various forms—worry about releasing the strategies and beliefs that served them well in the past, fear of additional work expectations, or anxiety about failure in front of their peers. In contrast, trailblazers in the organization envision significant growth and renewed energy with the advent of a change in direction. Both groups perceive obstacles to the implementation of the new approach and look to the leadership to remove any barriers. Thoughtful leaders facilitate conversations about the difficult challenge of change and address faculty and staff or parent fears and expectations. A part of the conversation includes inviting all groups within the organization to brainstorm viable solutions for removing barriers and maintaining the vision.

Case study leaders empowered faculty and staff and led them in defining possible impediments to making positive changes in teaching and learning. As faculty and staff struggled with interferences to making changes, their ownership of the new direction grew, and they developed solutions to the perceived obstacles. Tomlinson and the faculty of George Hall Elementary addressed specific obstacles seemingly out of their control. Barriers that interfered with students' school attendance sparked several innovations from the faculty, including providing uniforms for students in need and walking students home each day to ensure their safety and to deepen the school's relationship with the community.

Encouraging Conversations about New Ideas for Improvement

Forward thinking leaders create environments that encourage faculty and staff to search for ideas for improvement, while reinforcing the direction of the school or district at every opportunity. They challenge the status quo, and remind stakeholders "the definition of insanity is doing the same thing over and over again and expecting different results" (Einstein, n.d.). They also encourage faculty to look outside the norm for solutions and ensure that faculty understand failure is a possibility when attempting hard work.

Tips for Leaders

- Remind faculty and staff that taking a risk is often fear inducing, but groundbreaking resolutions or changes in practice do not occur without risks.
- Provide safety for those willing to risk for the sake of improved student learning.

CSD responded to community concerns about the level of student learning by involving them in the solution. Typically, principals, superintendents, and faculty work to attain *buy-in* among the many stakeholders for the direction and progress of the school and district. Superintendent Crumley envisioned a different strategy for effecting change within the district, a strategy that challenged the status quo. For Crumley, achieving *buy-in* was not enough. Crumley led a grass-roots effort to refocus the district and community on the essential skills and knowledge students must learn. Stakeholders from the business community, school district, local government, and parent community convened and dedicated themselves to the task of redesigning the focus and goals of the district. Crumley led stakeholders in developing and aligning to the state's essential standards the skills and knowledge relevant to the students and their community. The elimination of grade levels and the creation of a variety of authentic assessments gave voice to the community's wishes for their children.

The entire community created the new direction of the district; therefore, *buy-in* was not a concern. Instead, the community had *ownership* of the schools and district. Historically, if the work of schools and student learning did not meet the aspirations of the community, parents contacted the schools or central office. However, after the entire community collaborated on the creation of a new learning structure for the district, rather than pointing fingers or blaming the schools, everyone shared in the responsibility for making changes and ensuring student success. Community, faculty, and staff demonstrated renewed energy and commitment to supporting the district through the messy work of change and, as a result, guaranteed improved achievement.

CSD reevaluated every process, procedure, and curriculum so that students understood clearly the relevance of the information faculty asked them to learn. Crumley identified the work of the stakeholders as "outrageous thinking." The stakeholders took a risk and asked themselves *what are the students' interests, how can we connect the learning to the students,* and *how will we integrate the unique terrain and climate of our community with the required standards?* The conversations generated within the community groups prepared the way for a dynamic new culture of learning.

Implementing Methods to Motivate, Support, and/or Encourage Innovation

Effective leaders look to faculty to solve many of the obstacles to learning, help generate and celebrate new ideas, create a culture of innovation, and invest resources in innovation. Dr. Swann recalled taking a group of Bate Middle School faculty to the New York Consortium of Schools for professional development. At the end of the last day of training, Dr. Swann met with the group of participants while still on site to discuss any "take-aways" from the training. While still excited from the experience, the faculty mapped out next steps and action plans. "When teachers have power and input into the structure and work of the school, they go beyond anything I originally thought possible," Dr. Swann said. She encouraged innovation through Think Tank, where faculty innovation and suggestions prompted new ideas for the school. Faculty rotated through Think Tank throughout the day during release time from teaching. During Think Tank, faculty met with Dr. Swann and shared ideas, discussed new research, debated new strategies, and proposed new pathways of learning for students, faculty, and staff.

> What's really needed to foster breakthrough thinking and programs is a process that also rewards (and doesn't penalize) attempts to change and try new ideas, even if they don't work out as originally planned. If we just stay in the safe zone, fearing reprisal for failure, we're only serving to hinder the creation, development, and implementation of new ideas. Ideally, we should be celebrating not only successes, but failures.
>
> (Pohmer, n.d.)

Creating Opportunities for the Generation of New Ideas and Creation of Meaningful Change

Faculty at Bate Middle School also benefited from a weekly common collaborative time with Dr. Swann. Faculty and Swann struggled together in developing new strategies or formats and eliminating barriers to the teaching and learning process. Believing firmly that faculty had answers to many school problems or issues, Swann encouraged them to look beyond the usual solutions that continued a pattern of student mediocrity to strategies that "hooked" students in the experience and deepened the learning. Repeating outdated and ill-fitting strategies applies to schools as well as other organizations. Swann reminded faculty: "As educators, we often cannot find the simple solutions because we are so caught up in looking for the big solution." Swann led faculty to embrace the concept of turning from the old strategies of the past to newer and more authentic, real-life experiences. Bate's experiential, active learning format resulted in an increased depth of understanding and application in student learning.

Tips for Leaders

- Actively look for ways or occasions to encourage innovative thinking and change among the faculty and staff.
- Charge a faculty team with searching for new ideas and supporting change. Support the team with resources.
- Recognize, on a regular basis, new ideas implemented by faculty and staff.
- Continuously reframe problems into opportunities.

We are living in an era of extraordinary people rewriting our sense of what is possible. They make an unarguable case that a constraint should be regarded as a stimulus for positive change—we can choose to use it as an impetus to explore something new and arrive at a breakthrough. Not in spite of the constraint, but because of it.

(Morgan and Barden, 2015, Introduction, Section 4, para. 7)

Working with Others to Create a Culture of Innovation

Creating a capacity to innovate starts with strategy. The question then arises, Whose job is it to set this strategy? The answer is simple: the most senior leaders of the organization. Innovation cuts across just about every function. Only senior leaders can orchestrate such a complex system.

(Pisano, 2015, p. 54)

Innovative practice does not just happen. Genuine innovation requires the creation of a climate of trust, support, and encouragement, along with sensitivity to the fact that fear often accompanies change. Organizations and individuals often resist change. The forward thinking educational leader concentrates on creating a culture that reduces the fear of change and of failure. Leaders who support innovation also know that it is not enough to simply say, "Let's innovate." When innovation occurs in that way, it can be haphazard, misaligned with goals, and not supportive of the direction of the organization. Educators need to follow the example of high-performing business and health care organizations and *develop innovation strategies* that cover all operations of their organizations. Schools and districts might ask several questions to guide the development of an innovation strategy:

- What kinds of innovations will create the most value for our students?
- What kinds of innovations will create the most value for our stakeholders?
- What resources should these kinds of innovations receive?

Creation of an effective innovation strategy clearly requires visionary leadership and a collaborative culture. These case study leaders developed cultures of innovation and led faculty and staff in their schools and districts to take risks for the sake of deeper learning and to trust their colleagues for support.

Similar to many organizations, schools and districts include numerous facets that make up the whole but that function interdependently. A change in one part of the organization directly influences another part, which in turn causes a change in another part, and so on. School and district facets include student groups, faculty groups, parent groups, community groups, Board of Education groups, state and federal groups, and administrative groups. Innovative leaders anticipate the effects of change on each part or facet of the organization and consider the *snowball* effect of the proposed change or plan.

Tips for Leaders

- Lead faculty and staff in reading about the change process. Plan for possible interruptions in the process, and prepare for fears to arise as a reaction to change!
- Discuss the *elephant in the room* (fear of failure during change).
- Remind faculty and staff of the importance of trust as part of the collaborative process, and reinforce expectations of support among the group.

Thoughtful leaders, sensitive to faculty and staff feelings surrounding a change, create shared learning opportunities that assist in minimizing fears concerning changes. As faculty give voice to possible obstacles or fears of changes in teaching practice, the dialogue within the team strengthens the shared meaning and reduces anxiety.

When discussing a culture of innovation, Chugach School District's (CSD) Superintendent Crumley reiterated the point that empowerment and ownership fostered innovation as the district culture. Stakeholders who served as part of the process that built the new format for CSD experienced a level of involvement and belonging that surpassed typical school–community relationships and sent the message to all that *Chugach is not a business as usual school district.*

Celebrating New Ideas, Even If the Outcomes Are Not Always Successful

Committing oneself to a career of educating children is not for the faint of heart. The rewards of participating in opening a mind to a new concept or knowledge are without comparison. However, the day-to-day struggles of finding the key to learning for some students are sometimes discouraging and, occasionally, faculty feel the hard work of educating children goes unnoticed. Insightful leaders understand the enormity of the responsibilities associated with teaching and value public (and private) celebrations of faculty and staff success. "The extent to which the principal . . . recognizes and celebrates accomplishments and acknowledges failures" positively correlates with student achievement (Marzano et al., 2005, p. 42).

Tips for Leaders

- Celebrate successes and learn from one another.
- Celebrate failures. Use the failure as a learning tool for everyone.
- Model for the group the process of sharing an unsuccessful experience. Ask the group for suggestions to improve.
- Include internal and external stakeholders in designing and developing every innovation.

Recognition of their accomplishments validates the actions of faculty and staff and encourages them to continue in their quests for innovative strategies that bring learning to life for students. Forward-thinking leaders also appreciate the benefit of risk-taking and acknowledge that not every innovation will work. Accepting the fact that an innovation did not work is not an easy topic of discussion for anyone. As leaders share examples of their unsuccessful or failed experiences and seek input for possible next steps to improve experiences, they model for others the value of sharing failures and celebrating risk-taking. Faculty and staff gain comfort in attempting new strategies without fear of reprisal when leaders celebrate unsuccessful innovations. Knowledge that failures are also opportunities for learning provides faculty and staff with the self-assurance to attempt new strategies and removes a possible stigma associated with unsuccessful innovations.

Principal Swann recounted encouraging faculty to share their struggles with colleagues. She modeled and encouraged creative thinking as part of the business of leading students; yet, she recognized that not every initiative succeeded. Initially, faculty hesitated to discuss openly their unsuccessful learning experiences or initiatives; however, as Swann shared an unsuccessful experience of her own, faculty anxieties decreased about revealing their failed innovations. They responded to Swann's request for suggestions to help her avoid the same failure in other situations. As the discussion continued, the focus of the dialogue shifted from one of fear or embarrassment over a failure to one of support for a colleague and learning for everyone in the group. The take-away for the group in that discussion was that even ideas that are unsuccessful have at least one *pearl of wisdom* or valuable bit of new knowledge worth sharing.

Investing Resources in Supporting Innovation

Effective leaders understand the value of continuous learning and support to maintain the focus of the school or district. Naturally occurring barriers (budget constraints, varied interests, bureaucratic processes, changes in personnel) often interfere with sustaining innovation unless leaders are tenacious in their efforts to reinforce the direction and remove the barriers. Many schools and districts resist change, making more critical the need for leaders to identify resources that maintain the new initiatives. Supporting educational innovations that diverge from the traditional image of school requires investigation of resources or experiences that reinforce the innovation. Educators and stakeholders increasingly recognize the need for innovative approaches that improve student performance.

Tips for Leaders

- Collectively determine the resources that will support the innovations.
- Maintain a focus on the direction at all times.
- When faculty or staff request resources, ask if there is an innovative component in the request.

The superintendents and principals in these case studies recognized early in their careers the overwhelming need to find new ways to reach students. The avenue to reach their new goals included changes in the teaching and learning experiences. Each leader investigated and implemented the most appropriate resources. As the work grew, leaders guided faculty and staff in returning to their original Focus on Direction (Critical Practice 1) to maintain clarity of purpose. Leaders ensured that all resources supported the established emphases on collegial collaboration in creating deep learning experiences for students.

17 | **Conclusion**

Michael Fullan (2011, p. 24) identifies the work of effective leaders as a moral imperative and recognizes the hard work, seriousness, and tenacity involved in effecting positive and productive change in schools:

> We see here the moral imperative at its best—unwavering but respectful; unapologetically forthright but approachable; focused (on the goal and the practices to achieve it); sensitive to building capacity leadership in others; and celebrating success as a collective accomplishment.

The superintendents and principals highlighted in this book exemplify the description of effective leaders responding to the moral imperative to lead schools and districts in focusing on improved instructional practice.

In today's economic environment, organizations that do not respond to the rapidly changing global dynamics with actions and practices that work risk obsolescence. The educational community is in a similar situation. Students in the United States perform at lower academic levels than their international counterparts (Gonzales et al., 2008) and are an ongoing topic of the media, coffee shop, and ballpark conversations. The transformation of schools and districts into institutions of deep learning rather than places of compliance, low-level surface learning, and memorization requires communities, parents, faculty, staff, and students to shift their focus. The Five Critical Practices serve as a guide for superintendents and principals involved in the transformation process.

Discussions of student-focused teaching and learning often lead to side-conversations containing the questions "how does that look?" or "what identifiers signify that a school or district focuses on students and their learning?" The case studies in this book provide a sampling of *how it looks* and highlight the *identifiers that signify a focus on students and their learning.* Many other exemplary schools and districts share their secrets of accomplishing important work every day to equip students with the knowledge and skills necessary for success. Leaders recognize that the greatest desires of faculty and staff include raising the bar, closing the gap, meeting the standards, surpassing the benchmark, or the current imperative of the day. Educators arrive at work each day hoping to make a difference in the lives of students.

Great leaders are aware that the future begins every day, with every student, in every classroom and in every school. They know that it is their responsibility to help faculty capture the imagination of their students and inspire them to learn and reach for distant horizons beyond their current realities. Finally, great leaders realize that they only have the briefest of moments to accomplish their objectives. They know that their mission is to capture the student of today and to jump-start the leaders of tomorrow.

Appendix A: Data Analysis Tools

Affinity Diagram

http://www.isixsigma.com/tools-templates/affinity-diagram-kj-analysis/an-affinity-for-organized-thinking-a-diagram-with-many-uses/

Cause and Effect Diagram

http://asq.org/learn-about-quality/cause-analysis-tools/overview/fishbone.html

Check Sheet

http://www.processexcellencenetwork.com/lean-six-sigma-business-transformation/columns/the-check-sheet-a-simple-and-effective-way-to-disp/

Flowchart

http://www.mindtools.com/pages/article/newTMC_97.htm

Force Field Analysis

http://asq.org/service/body-of-knowledge/tools-force-field

Histogram

http://asq.org/learn-about-quality/data-collection-analysis-tools/overview/histogram.html

How-How Diagram

http://creatingminds.org/tools/how_how.htm

Nominal Group Technique
http://asq.org/learn-about-quality/idea-creation-tools/overview/nominal-group.html

Pareto Chart
http://asq.org/learn-about-quality/cause-analysis-tools/overview/pareto.html

Run Chart
http://asq.org/service/body-of-knowledge/tools-run-chart

Tree Diagram
http://asq.org/learn-about-quality/new-management-planning-tools/overview/tree-diagram.html

Appendix B: Five Critical Practices School or District Inventory

Always—regularly, continually, intentionally, formally, and informally; daily.
Often—regularly, consistently, intentionally, formally, and informally; at least weekly.
Sometimes—intentionally, formally, and informally; monthly.
Rarely—infrequently.
Never—not at all.

1: Focus on Direction

Standard	Always	Often	Sometimes	Rarely	Never
1.1 Creating an organizational culture					
We have positive and productive relationships with stakeholders.					
We participate in conversations among stakeholders.					
We participate in conversations and actions that build trust and support diversity.					
We demonstrate a shared culture of caring, communication, and collaboration.					

(Continued)

(Continued)

Standard	Always	Often	Sometimes	Rarely	Never
1.2 Working with others to support, encourage, or require high performance					
Our expectations promote high levels of performance in every area.					
Everyone* has actionable improvement goals.					
We use processes to monitor implementation of expectations and goals.					
Everyone receives feedback, direction, and support to strengthen performance.					
1.3 Using a vision, mission, and strategic plan to make decisions and inform actions					
Our mission, vision, and strategic plan reflect the beliefs, ethics, and focus of the organization.					
Our practices are consistent with the vision and mission and are based on the strategic plan.					
We look outside the norm for more effective ways of integrating the mission, vision, and strategic plan.					
We participate in conversations about vision and mission to support the direction of the organization.					

* Everyone includes leaders, faculty, staff, and students.

2: Build a Powerful Organization

Standard	Always	Often	Sometimes	Rarely	Never
2.1 Working with others to create a powerful organizational structure					
We collaborate to diagnose the current condition of the organization.					
We create and secure order.					
We participate with stakeholders in formal and informal conversations regarding the school or district environment.					
We collaborate with stakeholders to monitor the effectiveness of processes and procedures.					
2.2 Leading an organization in becoming agile and flexible					
We are engaged in reflective processes.					
We have risk-free opportunities to examine solutions to problems.					
We participate in open and professional dialogue to confront obstacles that stall progress.					
We take part in discussions with stakeholders for out-of-the-box answers to difficult problems.					

(Continued)

(Continued)

Standard	Always	Often	Sometimes	Rarely	Never
2.3 Leading others in developing, maintaining, and improving processes that increase the effectiveness of the organization					
We discuss performance effectiveness in all areas.					
We identify areas that matter most and are worth measuring.					
We accurately measure improvement in areas of most importance.					
We make mid-course adjustments for improvement.					

3: Ensure Student-Focused Vision and Action

Standard	Always	Often	Sometimes	Rarely	Never
3.1 Creating a vision and culture that focus on student learning and student needs					
We have a student-centered vision.					
Learning is the focus of student work.					
We develop processes that support student learning.					
We participate in maintaining a student learning focus.					

Standard	Always	Often	Sometimes	Rarely	Never
3.2 Providing instructional leadership					
Faculty experiences enhance learning for all.					
We participate in conversations regarding challenging, attainable learning experiences.					
Mutual respect among stakeholders is the norm.					
We demonstrate improvement in best teaching practices that result in high levels of learning.					
3.3 Leading the development of guidelines and procedures for learning					
We collaborate to design standards-based learning that addresses the variety of student needs.					
We provide active, experiential learning opportunities for students.					
We identify the essential skills and knowledge students must learn.					
We collaborate on lessons, units, and assessments.					

4: Give Life to Data

Standard	Always	Often	Sometimes	Rarely	Never
4.1 Ensuring that key data are analyzed in a deliberate manner					
We have access to data and information.					
We have regular opportunities to collaboratively analyze key data.					
We use effective tools to collaboratively analyze key data.					
Data analysis and use are reviewed on a regular basis.					
4.2 Using data and current research to improve student learning					
We participate in conversations about connections between teaching practices and student data.					
We develop teaching strategies in response to the data.					
We focus on recent research in the field and implications for instruction.					
The data that we use impact student learning.					

Standard	Always	Often	Sometimes	Rarely	Never
4.3 Communicating key data to all stakeholders					
Our data are transparent and clear.					
We have processes to deploy key data to stakeholders.					
Stakeholders understand key data.					
We communicate with stakeholders about data.					

5: Lead Learning

Standard	Always	Often	Sometimes	Rarely	Never
5.1 Establishing an environment of daily learning for all					
We collaborate, reflect, and share knowledge.					
Our focus is on learning rather than on teaching.					
Formal and informal collaboration and knowledge sharing are rewarded.					
We use systematic processes for sharing knowledge.					

(Continued)

(Continued)

5.2 Challenging the status quo and working with others to achieve change goals					
We invite different perspectives by asking the right questions and listening to the answers.					
We have a sense of urgency about positive change and improvement in every area.					
We are empowered to remove barriers to change.					
We participate in conversations about new ideas for improvement.					
5.3 Implementing methods to motivate, support, and/or encourage innovation					
We have opportunities to generate new ideas and create meaningful change.					
We collaborate in creating a culture of innovation.					
We celebrate new ideas, even if the outcomes are not always successful.					
We invest resources in supporting innovation.					

Appendix C: Five Critical Practices Framework

LEADERSHIP TEAM AND FACULTY LOOK FORS

Critical Practice 1: Focus on Direction

Leadership Team Look Fors	Faculty/Staff Look Fors
1.1 Creating an organizational culture	
Developing positive and productive relationships with stakeholders.	Nurturing positive and productive relationships with students, families, and colleagues.
Facilitating conversations among stakeholders.	Initiating and engaging in stakeholder conversations.
Encouraging and modeling conversations and actions that build trust and support diversity.	Modeling conversations and actions that build trust.
Creating a shared culture of caring, communication, and collaboration.	Demonstrating care, communication, and collaboration.
1.2 Working with others to support, encourage, or require high performance	
Setting expectations that promote high levels of performance in every area.	Creating common expectations within grade levels and across the school or district.
Ensuring that everyone has actionable improvement goals.	Writing and implementing improvement goals. Facilitating students' development of improvement goals.

(Continued)

(Continued)

Leadership Team Look Fors	Faculty/Staff Look Fors
Establishing processes to monitor implementation of expectations and goals.	Using processes to self-monitor implementation of expectations and goals. Modeling use of processes for self-monitoring.
Providing feedback, direction, and support to strengthen performance.	Reflecting and responding to feedback, direction, and support.
1.3 Using a vision, mission, and strategic plan to make decisions and inform actions	
Collaborating with others to develop a mission, vision, and strategic plan that reflect the beliefs, ethics, and focus of the organization.	Collaborating in developing and enacting the mission, vision, and strategic plan.
Ensuring that current and future practices are consistent with the vision and mission and are based on the strategic plan.	Ensuring that instructional practices are consistent with the vision and mission in the strategic plan.
Looking outside the norm for more effective ways of achieving the mission, vision, and strategic plan.	Participating in ongoing discussions and investigations, looking outside the norm for more effective ways of achieving the vision, mission, and strategic plan.
Leading conversations about vision and mission to support the direction of the organization.	Participating in conversations about vision and mission. Providing opportunities for students to discuss vision and mission.

Critical Practice 2: Build a Powerful Organization

Leadership Team Look Fors	Faculty/Staff Look Fors
2.1 Working with others to create a powerful organizational structure	
Diagnosing the current condition of the organization.	Collaborating and providing honest feedback about the current condition of the organization.
Creating and securing order.	Taking responsibility for creating and securing order within the school or district.

Leadership Team Look Fors	Faculty/Staff Look Fors
Engaging stakeholders in formal and informal conversations regarding the school or district environment.	Providing processes for students to participate in focused conversations regarding the school or district environment.
Collaborating with stakeholders to monitor the effectiveness of processes and procedures.	Monitoring and reporting the status and effectiveness of processes and procedures. Providing processes for students to report on the status of the school environment and effectiveness of processes and procedures.
2.2 Leading an organization in becoming agile and flexible	
Engaging others in reflective processes.	Engaging students and parents in reflective processes.
Creating risk-free opportunities to develop solutions to problems.	Providing a risk-free environment for students to engage in reflective processes, examine solutions, and share ideas.
Encouraging open and professional dialogue to confront obstacles that stall progress.	Providing honest and professional feedback concerning obstacles that stall progress.
Engaging stakeholders in discussions for out-of-the-box answers to difficult problems.	Initiating and engaging in discussion to provide out-of-the-box answers to difficult problems.
2.3 Leading others in developing, maintaining, and improving processes that increase the effectiveness of the organization	
Engaging stakeholders in discussions of performance effectiveness in all areas.	Providing feedback about performance effectiveness. Providing opportunities for students to discuss performance effectiveness.
Identifying areas that matter most and are worth measuring.	Participating in discussions about areas that matter most and are worth measuring.

(Continued)

(Continued)

Leadership Team Look Fors	Faculty/Staff Look Fors
Engaging others in accurately measuring improvement in areas identified as most important.	Collaborating to identify and develop processes and tools that accurately measure improvement in areas previously highlighted as most important.
Leading others in making mid-course adjustments for improvement.	Analyzing data to make mid-course adjustments for continuous improvement. Gathering feedback from students regarding mid-course adjustments.

Critical Practice 3: Ensure Student-Focused Vision and Action

Leadership Team Look Fors	Faculty/Staff Look Fors
3.1 Creating a vision and culture that focus on student learning and student needs	
Leading stakeholders in crafting a student-centered vision.	Engaging with others in crafting a student-centered vision. Articulating and demonstrating the vision in daily experiences. Facilitating student input in the development of visions, goals, and expectations for learning.
Ensuring that learning is the focus of student work.	Reviewing the effectiveness of actions related to student focus.
Facilitating the development of processes that support student learning.	Participating in ongoing professional learning that supports processes for student learning.
Leading faculty and staff in maintaining a focus on student learning.	Engaging in self-monitoring and peer monitoring of practices that maintain a student learning focus (such as collegial conversations, observations, lesson study).

Leadership Team Look Fors	Faculty/Staff Look Fors
3.2 Providing instructional leadership	
Coordinating faculty and staff experiences that enhance learning for all.	Coordinating and engaging in continuous learning experiences. Providing engaging learning experiences for students.
Facilitating conversations regarding challenging, attainable learning experiences.	Initiating and participating in collegial conversations. Providing time and space for students to engage in focused instructional conversations with peers.
Modeling and encouraging mutual respect among stakeholders.	Demonstrating respect for varying opinions. Providing time and space for conversations and conferences with students.
Ensuring growth in best teaching practices that result in high levels of learning.	Initiating discussions and implementation of best teaching practices.
3.3 Leading the development of guidelines and procedures for learning	
Leading the design of standards-based learning that addresses the variety of student needs.	Investigating, creating, implementing, and evaluating standards-based learning.
Ensuring the development of active, experiential learning opportunities for students.	Investigating, creating, implementing, and evaluating standards-based learning that is active and experiential.
Facilitating an identification of essential skills and knowledge students must learn.	Continuously reflecting and analyzing within and across grade levels the content students must know and need to be able to do.
Creating opportunities for faculty to collaborate on lessons, units, and assessments.	Effectively using the time allocated to collaborate on student needs and meeting standards.

Critical Practice 4: Give Life to Data

Leadership Team Look Fors	Faculty/Staff Look Fors
4.1 Ensuring that key data are analyzed in a deliberate manner	
Ensuring the availability of data and information.	Providing feedback on data and information provided.
Providing regular opportunities to collaboratively analyze key data.	Effectively using the allocated time for data analysis. Providing opportunities for students to analyze data.
Ensuring the use of effective tools to collaboratively analyze key data.	Providing honest and open feedback on data analysis tools. Identifying barriers to collaborative work and sharing with leadership.
Reviewing data analysis and use on a regular basis.	Participating in data analysis and use. Providing opportunities for students to analyze and use data.
4.2 Using data and current research to improve student learning	
Facilitating faculty and staff conversations about connections between teaching practices and student data.	Participating in and *initiating* dialogue relevant to actual practices and student data. Providing time and space to listen to and learn from students about their content learning (such as exit slips, conferences).
Ensuring the development of teaching strategies in response to the data.	Using professional learning opportunities to identify needs based on data, evaluate practices, and implement revised and/or additional strategies when appropriate. Using student voice as a key data point.
Focusing on recent research in the field and implications for instruction.	Participating in conversations, investigating research, and studying implications through actual classroom practices.
Ensuring that data used impact student learning.	Using relevant data to make a positive difference in student learning.

Leadership Team Look Fors	Faculty/Staff Look Fors
4.3 Communicating key data to all stakeholders	
Ensuring transparency and clarity of the data.	Providing feedback about transparency and clarity of data.
Establishing processes to deploy key data to stakeholders.	Deploying data to stakeholders based on established processes.
Developing stakeholder understanding of key data.	Using the disaggregated data to develop common understandings and to discuss openly the implications for practice. Developing a process for students to reflect on their understanding of key data.
Communicating with stakeholders about data.	Clearly articulating the implications of the data across the school or district.

Critical Practice 5: Lead Learning

Leadership Team Look Fors	Faculty/Staff Look Fors
5.1 Establishing an environment of daily learning for all	
Modeling collaboration, reflection, and knowledge sharing in daily practice.	Effectively utilizing the protected time for knowledge sharing every day.
Leading a shift from a focus on teaching to a focus on learning.	Reviewing lessons and student results to make sure the focus is on learning. Continuously creating time and space for students to collaborate, reflect, and share.
Rewarding formal and informal collaboration and knowledge sharing.	Maximizing formal and informal opportunities for collaboration. Providing opportunities for student knowledge sharing.
Maintaining systematic processes for sharing knowledge.	Sharing knowledge using systematic processes. Developing processes for student knowledge sharing.

(Continued)

(Continued)

Leadership Team Look Fors	Faculty/Staff Look Fors
5.2 Challenging the status quo and working with others to achieve change goals	
Inviting different perspectives from others by asking the right questions and listening to the answers.	Providing honest opinions and feedback. Inviting different perspectives from students.
Creating a sense of urgency about positive change and improvement in every area.	Identifying issues that need positive change and initiating discussions about the issues.
Empowering others to remove barriers to change.	Initiating the removal of barriers to change that interfere with learning.
Encouraging conversations about new ideas for improvement.	Initiating and engaging in conversations about new ideas with colleagues and students.
5.3 Implementing methods to motivate, support, and/or encourage innovation	
Creating opportunities for the generation of new ideas and creation of meaningful change.	Engaging in professional learning communities that focus on studying, implementing, and evaluating new ideas and the resulting changes. Providing time and space for students to utilize the new practices.
Working with others to create a culture of innovation.	Collaboratively developing processes that support the study, implementation, and evaluation of innovations. Including students in the development of new ideas and processes.
Celebrating new ideas, even if the outcomes are not always successful.	Initiating and recognizing new ideas. Supporting student design of new ideas.
Investing resources in supporting innovation.	Requesting and using resources for the implementation of innovative programs and practices.

References

Aaker, D. (2012, January 5). The genius bar: Branding the innovation. *Harvard Business Review*. Retrieved from https://hbr.org/2012/01/the-genius-bar-branding-the-in

Allensworth, E., and Easton, J.Q. (2005). *The on-track indicator as a predictor of high school graduation*. Chicago, IL: Consortium on Chicago School Research.

Annenberg Institute for School Reform. (2004). Professional learning communities: Professional development strategies that improve instruction. Retrieved from http://www.annenberginstitute.org/pdf/ProfLearning.pdf

Arum, R. (2003). *Judging school discipline: The crisis of moral authority*. Cambridge, MA: Harvard University Press.

Bernhardt, V. (2004). *Data analysis for continuous school improvement* (2nd ed.). Larchmont, NY: Routledge (Eye on Education).

BNQP (Baldrige National Quality Program). (2008). Award Recipient Iredell-Statesville Schools. Gaithersburg, MD: U.S. Department of Commerce, National Institute of Standards and Technology. Retrieved from http://www.nist.gov/baldrige/publications/upload/Iredell_Statesville_Schools_Profile.pdf

Bryk, A.S., and Schneider, B. (2002). *Trust in schools: A core resource for improvement*. New York, NY: Russell Sage Foundation.

Carroll, L. (2004). *Alice in wonderland*. New York, NY: Gramercy Publishing

Deal, T., and Peterson, K. (1999). *Shaping school culture: The heart of leadership*. San Francisco, CA: Jossey-Bass.

The Digital Universe of Opportunities: Rich data and the increasing value of the internet of things. (2014, April). Retrieved from http://uk.emc.com/leadership/digital-universe/2014iview/index.htm

Dorfman, D., and Fisher, A. (2002). Building relationships for student success: School–family–community partnerships and student achievement in the Northwest. Portland, OR: Northwest Regional Educational Laboratory. Retrieved from http://www.nwrel.org/partnerships/pubs/building.html

Duncan, A. (2010, December 7). Remarks at OECD's release of the program for international student assessment (PISA) 2009. Annual meeting of senior officials from centres of government on ensuring the coherence of reform: Steering from the centre of government, OECD headquarters, Paris, France. Retrieved from http://www.ed.gov/news/speeches/secretary-arne-duncans-remarks-oecds-release-program-international-student-assessment-

Fullan, M. (2001). *Leading in a culture of change.* San Francisco, CA: Jossey-Bass.

Fullan, M. (2011). *The moral imperative realized.* Thousand Oaks, CA: Corwin.

Gonzales, P., Williams, T., Jocelyn, L., Roey, S., Kastberg, D., and Brenwald, S. (2008). *Highlights from TIMSS 2007: Mathematics and science achievement of U.S. fourth-and eighth-grade students in an international context.* Washington, DC: National Center for Education Statistics, Institute of Education Sciences, U.S. Department of Education.

Harvard Family Research Project. (2010). *Partnerships for learning: Profiles of three school–community partnership efforts.* Retrieved from http://www.hfrp.org/out-of-school-time/publications-resources/partnerships-for-learning-profiles-of-three-school-community-partnership-efforts

Heifetz, R., and Laurie, D. (1997). The work of leadership. *Harvard Business Review,* 75(1), 124–134.

Henderson, A., and Mapp, K. (2002). *A new wave of evidence: The impact of school, family and community connections on student achievement.* Austin, TX: Southwest Educational Development Laboratory (SEDL). Retrieved from http://www.sedl.org/ connections/resources/evidence

Horwath, R. (2009). *Deep dive: The proven method for building strategy, focusing your resources and taking smart action.* Austin, TX: Greenleaf Group Press.

Interstate School Leaders Licensure Consortium. (2012). ISLLC standards. Retrieved from http://coe.fgcu.edu/faculty/valesky/isllcstandards.htm

Iredell-Statesville Schools. (2015). Baldrige 2008 application. Retrieved from http://iss.schoolwires.com//site/Default.aspx?PageID=1450

Kaplan, C., and Chan, R. (2011). *Time well spent: Eight powerful practices of successful, expanded-time schools.* Boston, MA: National Center on Time & Learning.

Kaplan, C., Chan, R., Farbman, D., and Novoryta, A. (2014). *Time for teachers: Leveraging time to strengthen instruction and empower teachers.* Boston, MA: National Center on Time & Learning.

Kearney, W., Kelsey, C., and Herrington, D. (2013). *Mindful leaders in highly effective schools: A mixed-method application of Hoy's m-scale.* Thousand Oaks, CA: SAGE Publications.

Kotter, J. (1996). *Leading change.* Boston, MA: Harvard Business School Press.

Kotter, J., and Cohen, D. (2002). *The heart of change: Real-life stories of how people change their organizations.* Boston, MA: Harvard Business School Press.

Lacoe, J. (2013). Too scared to learn? The academic consequences of feeling unsafe at school. Institute for Education and Social Policy, Working Paper Series. Retrieved from http://steinhardt.nyu.edu/scmsAdmin/media/users/ggg5/Working_Paper_02-13.pdf

Leana, C.R. (2011, Fall). The missing link in school reform. *Stanford Social Innovation Review.* Retrieved from http://www.ssireview.org/articles/entry/the_missing_link_in_school_reform

Lee, L., and Zimmerman, M. (n.d.). *Passion, action and a new vision for student voice: Learnings from the Manitoba School Improvement Program.* Winnipeg, Canada: The Manitoba School Improvement Program, Inc.

Leithwood, K., Louis, K.S., Anderson, S., and Wahlstrom, K. (2004). *How leadership influences student learning.* New York: The Wallace Foundation.

Liedtka, J. (1998). Strategic thinking: Can it be taught? *Long Range Planning,* 31(1), 120–129.

McFillen, J.M., O'Neil, D.A., Balzer, W.K., and Varney, G.H. (2013). Organizational diagnosis: An evidenced-based approach. *Journal of Change Management,* 13(2), 223–246.

Marzano, R., Waters, T., and McNulty, B.A. (2005). *School leadership that works: From research to results.* Alexandria, VA: Association for Supervision and Curriculum Development; Aurora, CO: Mid-continent Research for Education and Learning.

Merrill, P. (2015). A brief history of quality. *Quality Progress*, 48(5), 42–44.

Montalvo, G.P., Mansfield, E.A., and Miller, R.B. (2007). Liking or disliking the teacher: Student motivation, engagement and achievement. *Evaluation and Research in Education*, 20(3), 144–158. Retrieved from http://dx.doi.org/10.2167/eri406.0

Morgan, A., and Barden, M. (2015). *A beautiful constraint: How to turn your limitations into advantages, and why it's everyone's business.* Hoboken, NJ: John Wiley & Sons, Inc. Kindle iPad version. Retrieved from www.amazon.com

National Association of Elementary School Principals. (2008). *Leading learning communities: Standards for what principals should know and be able to do. Executive summary.* Retrieved from http://www.naesp.org/resources/1/Pdfs/LLC2-ES.pdf

National Association of Secondary School Principals. (2010). *Breaking ranks: 10 skills for successful school leaders executive summary.* Retrieved from http://www.nassp.org/Content/158/BR_tenskills_ExSum.pdf

National Association of Secondary School Principals. (2012). *2013 MetLife Foundation–NASSP Breakthrough Schools.* Retrieved from http://www.nassp.org/Awards-and-Recognition/Breakthrough-Schools/Breakthrough-Schools-Past-and-Present/2013-MetLife-Foundation-NASSP-Breakthrough-Schools

National Association of Secondary School Principals. (2013). *2014 MetLife Foundation–NASSP Breakthrough Schools.* Retrieved from http://www.nassp.org/Awards-and-Recognition/Breakthrough-Schools/Breakthrough-Schools-Past-and-Present/2014-MetLife-Foundation-NASSP-Breakthrough-Schools

National Association of Secondary School Principals. (2014a). Great schools have great principals. *Principal Leadership*, 14. Retrieved from http://www.nassp.org/tabid/3788/default.aspx?topic=Great_Schools_Have_Great_Principals_PL0514

National Association of Secondary School Principals. (2014b). Sharing responsibility and results. *Principal Leadership*, 14. Retrieved from

http://www.principals.org/tabid/3788/default.aspx?topic=Sharing_
Responsibility_and_Results

Organization for Economic Co-operation and Development. (2012). *Country note: United States.* Retrieved from: http://www.oecd.org/pisa/keyfindings/pisa-2012-results.htm

Page, S. (2008). *The difference: How the power of diversity creates better groups, firms, schools and societies.* Princeton, NJ: Princeton University Press.

Pewaukee School District. (2015). Baldrige 2013 application. Retrieved from http://wi-forwardbaldrige-quali.pewaukeeschools.schoolfusion.us/modules/locker/files/group_files.phtml?parent=13026498&gid=2959116&sessionid=733b829fcc0a0a0c5de29a400c9e6fd5

Pisano, G.P. (2015). You need an innovation strategy. *Harvard Business Review*, 93(6), 44–54.

Pohmer, S. (n.d.). Pohmer on . . . celebrate . . . failures. Retrieved from http://www.lgrmag.com/pohmer-oncelebrate%E2%80%A6failures

Raymond, L. (2001). Student involvement in school improvement: From data source to significant voice. *FORUM*, 43(2), 58–61.

Reeves, D.B. (2009). *Leading change in your school.* Alexandria, VA: ASCD.

Romero, M., and Lee, Y. (2007). *A national portrait of chronic absenteeism in the early grades.* New York, NY: The National Center for Children in Poverty.

Schlechty, P. (2002). *Working on the work: An action plan for teachers, principals, and superintendents.* San Francisco, CA: Jossey-Bass.

Schlechty, P. (2005). Creating the capacity to support innovations (Occasional Paper #2). Louisville, KY: Schlechty Center for Leadership in School Reform. Retrieved from www.schlechtycenter.org/pdfs/supportinn.pdf

Schlechty, P. (2009). *Leading for learning: How to transform schools into learning organizations.* San Francisco, CA: Jossey-Bass.

Southern Regional Education Board. (2010). *SREB learning-centered leadership program: Developing and assisting effective learning-centered principals who can improve schools and increase student achievement.* Retrieved from http://www.sreb.org/uploads/documents/2010/06/2010060210530329/2010_Program_Booklet.pdf

Valentine, J., Clark, D., Hackmann, D., and Petzko, V. (2004). *Leadership for highly successful middle level schools, volume 2: A national study of leadership in middle level schools*. Reston, VA: National Association of Secondary School Principals.

Wallace Foundation. (2012). *The school principal as leader: Guiding schools to better teaching and learning*. Retrieved from www.wall acefoundation.org/knowledge-center/school-leadership/effective-principal-leadership/Pages/The-School-Principal-as-Leader-Guiding-Schools-to-Better-Teaching-and-Learning.aspx

Waters, J.T., Cameron, G., Melver, M., Eck, J., Kearns, J., Seebaum, M., et al. (2009). *Balanced leadership: School level leadership—An overview (facilitators' manual)*. Denver, CO: Mid-continent Research for Education and Learning (McREL).

Waters, J.T., and Marzano, R.J. (2007). School district leadership that works: The effect of superintendent leadership on student achievement. *ERS Spectrum*, 25(2), 1–12.

Waters, J.T., Marzano, R.J., and McNulty, B. (2003). *Balanced leadership: What 30 years of research tells us about the effect of leadership on student achievement*. Aurora, CO: McREL.

Wyner, J., Dilulio, J., and Bridgeland, J. (2007). *Achievementrap: How America is failing millions of higher achieving students from lower income families*. Washington, DC: Civic Enterprises.

Personal Communications

Alice Ott Middle School, James Johnston, principal—March 20, 2015.

Bate Middle School, Amy Swann, principal—November 13, 2014.

Chugach School District, Bob Crumley, superintendent—March 16, 2015; April 13, 2015.

Chugach School District, Debbie Treece, K.I.D. Coordinator—March 16, 2015; April 13, 2015.

Deer Valley Elementary School, Wayne Richardson, principal—November 20, 2014.

Frank M. Silvia Elementary School, Denise Ward, principal—July 2, 2015.

Garner Magnet High School, Drew Cook, principal—July 14, 2015.

George Hall Elementary School, Terri Tomlinson, principal—June 11, 2012.

Hastings Middle School, David Essink, principal—July 3, 2015.

Hewitt-Trussville Middle School, Phyllis Faust, principal—October 17, 2012.

Iredell-Statesville School District, Brady Johnson, superintendent—July 8, 2015.

Kennedy Elementary School, Montie Koehn, principal—February 2, 2015.

Maplewood Richmond Heights High School, Kevin Grawer, principal—March 4, 2015.

Mountain Brook School District, Charles Mason, superintendent—July 8, 2015.

Pewaukee School District, JoAnn Sternke, superintendent—December 16, 2014.

Pike Road School District, Suzanne Freeman, superintendent—April 23, 2015.

Robert M. Finley Middle School, Aneal Alston, principal—December 18, 2014.

Scott Morgan Johnson Middle School, Mitchell Curry, principal—July 7, 2015.

Trenton High School, Dan Wiebers, principal—July 2, 2015.

Winston Campus Elementary School, Andy Tieman, principal—July 2, 2015.

Winterboro High School, Craig Bates, principal—September 11, 2012.